Luscious I Cakes: 103 Recipes to Satisfy Your Sweet Tooth

The Blue Dolphin Koid

Copyright © 2023 The Blue Dolphin Koid
All rights reserved.
:

Contents

INTRODUCTION 7
1. classic lemon cake 9
2. lemon bundt cake 10
3. lemon pound cake 11
4. lemon layer cake 12
5. lemon blueberry cake 13
6. lemon raspberry cake 14
7. lemon poppy seed cake 15
8. lemon chiffon cake 16
9. lemon sponge cake 18
10. lemon meringue cake 19
11. lemon cream cheese cake 20
12. lemon yogurt cake 21
13. lemon olive oil cake 22
14. lemon coconut cake 23
15. lemon honey cake 24
16. lemon ginger cake 25
17. lemon lavender cake 26
18. strawberry lemon cake 27
19. lemon rose cake 29
20. lemon apple cake 30
21. lemon almond cake 31
22. lemon cardamom cake 32
23. lemon thyme cake 33
24. lemon lime cake 34
25. lemon banana cake 35
26. lemon carrot cake 36
27. lemon cranberry cake 37

28. lemon apricot cake 38
29. lemon fig cake 40
30. lemon hazelnut cake 41
31. lemon peach cake 42
32. lemon pistachio cake 43
33. lemon plum cake 44
34. lemon rum cake 45
35. lemon sesame cake 46
36. lemon tea cake 47
37. lemon walnut cake 48
38. blueberry lemon ricotta cake 49
39. lemon cherry cake 50
40. lemon matcha cake 51
41. lemon orange cake 52
42. lemon blackberry cake 53
43. lemon elderflower cake 55
44. lemon fig and goat cheese cake 56
45. lemon chestnut cake 57
46. lemon sweet potato cake 58
47. lemon zucchini cake 59
48. lemon chocolate cake 60
49. lemon date cake 61
50. lemon gingerbread cake 63
51. lemon cranberry upside-down cake 64
52. lemon lavender almond cake 65
53. lemon macadamia nut cake 66
54. lemon orange almond cake 67
55. lemon polenta cake 68
56. lemon pumpkin cake 70

57. lemon semolina cake 71
58. lemon strawberry shortcake 71
59. lemon white chocolate cake 73
60. lemon blueberry cream cheese cake 74
61. lemon chamomile cake 75
62. lemon coconut cream cake 77
63. lemon elderflower and raspberry cake 77
64. lemon and lavender honey cake 78
65. lemon matcha pound cake 79
66. lemon olive oil and thyme cake 81
67. lemon peanut butter cake 82
68. lemon poppyseed bundt cake 83
69. lemon raspberry cream cake 84
70. lemon gingerbread bundt cake 86
71. lemon and rosemary olive oil cake 87
72. lemon and strawberry parfait cake 88
73. lemon blackberry and honey cake 89
74. lemon coconut and mango cake 90
75. lemon and orange upside-down cake 92
76. lemon buttermilk cake 93
77. lemon and pistachio pound cake 94
78. lemon and ricotta cake 95
79. lemon and strawberry marble cake 96
80. lemon and white chocolate bundt cake 97
81. lemon and raspberry drizzle cake 98
82. lemon and elderflower drizzle cake 99
83. lemon and blueberry custard cake 100
84. lemon and thyme drizzle cake 102
85. lemon and poppyseed layer cake 103

86. vegan lemon cake 104

87. gluten-free lemon cake 105

88. paleo lemon cake 107

89. keto lemon cake 108

90. low-fat lemon cake 109

91. lemon and lime drizzle bundt cake 110

92. lemon and rosemary cake with mascarpone frosting 111

93. lemon and basil olive oil cake 112

94. lemon and blackberry yogurt cake 113

95. lemon and carrot bundt cake 114

96. lemon and coconut bundt cake 115

97. lemon and grapefruit drizzle cake 117

98. lemon and lavender pound cake 118

99. lemon and raspberry swirl cake 119

100. lemon and thyme polenta cake 121

101. lemon and white chocolate layer cake with raspberry filling 122

102. lemon ricotta bundt cake 123

103. lemon and strawberry cream cheese pound cake 124

CONCLUSION 126

INTRODUCTION

Looking for a cookbook that will satisfy your sweet tooth while leaving a tangy taste on your palate? Look no further than "Luscious Lemon Cakes" – the ultimate collection of 103 delectable and easy-to-make lemon cake recipes.

Lemon cakes have always been a crowd-pleaser, whether they're light and creamy or dense and tart. Their bold flavor and fresh scent make them a perfect choice for any occasion – from a summery picnic or afternoon tea, to a formal dessert after a dinner party or special occasion.

The recipes in this cookbook are diverse, featuring a wide range of textures, flavors and styles, so you can find the perfect lemon cake recipe for every occasion. Whether you prefer a light and fluffy lemon sponge cake or a rich, indulgent lemon pound cake, you'll find plenty of options to choose from.

This cookbook is written for home bakers of all skill levels, so you don't need to be an expert in the kitchen to create these fantastic lemon cakes. Each recipe is clearly explained, with step-by-step instructions to guide you through the process. You'll also find helpful tips and tricks throughout the book to make sure every cake you bake comes out perfectly.

For those who love to experiment and customize their recipes, "Luscious Lemon Cakes" has plenty of opportunities to do so. Variation notes accompany each recipe, providing different ways to modify or adapt existing recipes. You can add a touch of vanilla, swap out one ingredient for another or increase/decrease the quantity of any ingredient. The possibilities are endless, so don't be afraid to get creative in the kitchen.

With "Luscious Lemon Cakes," you'll get more than just 103 delicious lemon cake recipes – you'll also get a deeper understanding of the art and science of baking. The book will take you through the fundamentals of baking, with tips on ingredient selection, baking equipment and techniques, as well as an explanation of how different ingredients work together to create different textures and flavors.

So whether you're a seasoned home baker or just starting out, "Luscious Lemon Cakes" is the perfect cookbook to add to your collection. With its wide range of delicious and easy-to-make lemon cake recipes, it's sure to become a staple in your kitchen.

1. classic lemon cake

Classic Lemon Cake
Serving: 8-10
Preparation Time: 15 minutes
Ready Time: 50 minutes

Ingredients:
- 2 1/2 cups all-purpose flour
- 1/2 teaspoon baking powder
- 1/4 teaspoon baking soda
- 1/4 teaspoon salt
- 3 eggs
- 2 cups granulated sugar
- 2 teaspoons grated lemon zest
- 3/4 cup vegetable oil
- 3/4 cup lemon juice
- 1/2 cup sour cream

Instructions:
1. Preheat oven to 350° F. Grease and flour a 9x13 inch baking pan.
2. In a medium bowl, combine flour, baking powder, baking soda and salt.
3. In a large bowl, beat eggs, then add sugar and lemon zest. Beat until light and fluffy.
4. Gradually add oil and lemon juice, beating until combined.
5. Add dry Ingredients to wet Ingredients, mixing just until combined.
6. Gently stir in sour cream.
7. Pour into prepared pan and bake for 40-50 minutes, or until a toothpick inserted in the center comes out clean.
8. Let cool before serving.

Nutrition Information:
Calories: 358
Fat: 11.4 g
Saturated Fat: 2 g
Carbohydrates: 57.3 g
Fiber: 0.6 g

Protein: 4.1 g
Sodium: 161.3 mg

2. lemon bundt cake

This classic lemon bundt cake is deliciously moist, light, and sweet - the perfect dessert or tea cake. It is zesty, light, and the perfect finish to any meal.

Serving:
Serves 10-12 people
Preparation Time:
15 minutes
Ready Time:
1 hour 15 minutes

Ingredients:
- 4 eggs, at room temperature
- 2 ½ cups all-purpose flour
- 2 teaspoons baking powder
- ¼ teaspoon salt
- 1 ½ cups (3 sticks) unsalted butter, at room temperature
- 2 cups granulated sugar
- zest of 4 large lemons
- ½ teaspoon pure lemon extract
- ¾ cup whole milk

Instructions:
1. Preheat the oven to 350°F and lightly grease a bundt cake pan.
2. In a medium sized bowl, whisk together the flour, baking powder and salt.
3. In the bowl of a stand mixer, beat the butter and sugar until light and fluffy.
4. Add the eggs, one at a time, beating well after each addition.
5. Add the lemon zest and lemon extract and mix until combined.
6. With the mixer on low speed, add the flour mixture in three additions, alternating with the milk. Beat just until combined.
7. Pour the batter into the prepared pan and bake for 55 to 60 minutes, or until a toothpick inserted into the center comes out clean.

8. Allow the cake to cool in the pan for 10 minutes before inverting it onto a wire rack to cool completely.

Nutrition Information:
Amount Per Serving (1 piece):
Calories: 325 kcal, Carbohydrates: 47 g, Protein: 4 g, Fat: 14 g, Saturated Fat: 8 g, Cholesterol: 84 mg, Sodium: 136 mg, Potassium: 96 mg, Fiber: 1 g, Sugar: 29 g, Vitamin A: 487 IU, Vitamin C: 2 mg, Calcium: 67 mg, Iron: 1 mg

3. lemon pound cake

Lemon Pound Cake
A classic pound cake made with a zesty lemon flavor, this Lemon Pound Cake is sure to become a family favorite!
Serving: 8
Preparation Time: 20 minutes
Ready Time: 1 hour 25 minutes

Ingredients:
- 1 cup butter, softened
- 2 cups white sugar
- 4 eggs, at room temperature
- 1 teaspoon vanilla extract
- 1/4 cup freshly squeezed lemon juice
- 2 tablespoons lemon zest
- 3 cups all-purpose flour
- 1/2 teaspoon baking powder
- 1/2 teaspoon salt
- 2/3 cup milk, at room temperature
- Powdered sugar for dusting (optional)

Instructions:
1. Preheat oven to 350 degrees F (175 degrees C). Grease and flour 10-inch tube or bundt pan.
2. In a large bowl, cream together butter and sugar until light and fluffy. Beat in eggs one at a time. Add in vanilla, lemon juice, and lemon zest and mix until combined.

3. In a separate bowl, sift together flour, baking powder, and salt. Add dry Ingredients to wet Ingredients alternately with milk, mixing just until combined.

4. Pour batter into prepared pan and bake in preheated oven until a toothpick inserted into the center of the cake comes out clean, about 1 hour and 5 minutes. Allow cake to cool in pan for 10 minutes, then remove from pan and continue cooling on a wire rack. Once completely cool, dust with powdered sugar and serve.

Nutrition Information:
Calories: 362; Total Fat: 12.6g; Cholesterol: 80mg; Sodium: 210mg; Total Carbohydrates: 56.7g; Dietary Fiber: 1.3g; Protein: 6.2g

4. lemon layer cake

Lemon Layer Cake
Serving: 12 servings
Preparation time: 30 minutes
Ready time: 2 hours

Ingredients:
- 2 ½ cups all-purpose flour
- 2 teaspoons baking powder
- ¼ teaspoon baking soda
- ½ teaspoon salt
- ½ cup butter, softened
- 2 cups granulated sugar
- 4 large eggs
- 1 ½ teaspoons pure vanilla extract
- 1 cup sour cream
- Juice and zest of 2 lemons
- 2 ¼ cups confectioners' sugar

Instructions:
1. Preheat oven to 350°F. Grease two 9-inch round cake pans with butter and set aside.
2. In a medium bowl, whisk together flour, baking powder, baking soda, and salt.

3. In a large bowl, use an electric mixer to beat together the butter and sugar until light and fluffy.
4. Beat in eggs, one at a time, then stir in vanilla.
5. Add flour mixture to the butter mixture and mix until just combined.
6. Mix in the sour cream, lemon juice, and lemon zest until fully incorporated.
7. Divide the cake batter evenly between the prepared pans.
8. Bake for 25-30 minutes, until a toothpick inserted into the center of the cake comes out clean. Allow to cool for 15 minutes, then remove from the pans and cool completely before frosting.
9. To make the frosting, mix together the confectioners' sugar and lemon juice in a medium bowl. Adjust as needed to reach desired consistency.
10. Spread frosting over the cooled cakes and serve.

Nutrition Information (per serving):
Calories: 347 kcal, Carbohydrates: 51 g, Protein: 4 g, Fat: 14 g, Saturated Fat: 8 g, Cholesterol: 76 mg, Sodium: 148 mg, Potassium: 102 mg, Fiber: 1 g, Sugar: 36 g, Vitamin A: 457 IU, Vitamin C: 4 mg, Calcium: 48 mg, Iron: 1 mg

5. lemon blueberry cake

This moist and flavorful lemon blueberry cake is a delightful way to satisfy your sweet tooth. Bursting with sweet and tart citrus flavors and then topped with fresh, juicy blueberries, this cake is sure to please.
Serving: 8
Preparation Time: 25 minutes
Ready Time: 1 hour

Ingredients:
- 1/2 cup butter, softened
- 1 1/2 cups granulated sugar
- 2 eggs
- 2 cups all-purpose flour
- 2 teaspoons baking powder
- 1 teaspoon salt
- 2/3 cup milk
- 1/4 cup freshly squeezed lemon juice

- 2 tablespoons lemon zest
- 1 teaspoon vanilla extract
- 1 cup fresh blueberries

Instructions:
1. Preheat the oven to 350 degrees F. Grease a 9-inch round cake pan.
2. In a medium bowl, cream the butter and sugar together until light and fluffy. Add the eggs one at a time, mixing until fully incorporated.
3. In a separate bowl, sift together the flour, baking powder and salt.
4. Alternating between the dry Ingredients and the milk, add the dry Ingredients and the milk to the butter and sugar mixture in three batches. Mix until just combined.
5. Add the lemon juice, zest and vanilla extract and mix until fully incorporated.
6. Gently fold in the blueberries until evenly distributed.
7. Pour the batter into the cake pan and bake for 40-45 minutes, or until a toothpick inserted in the center comes out clean. Allow the cake to cool before serving.

Nutrition Information:
Per Serving: 280 Calories, 11g Fat, (6g Saturated Fat), 42g Carbohydrates, (20.5g Sugar), 3g Fiber, 4g Protein, 135mg Sodium

6. lemon raspberry cake

This zesty Lemon Raspberry Cake is a delicious example of what happens when two wonderful flavors come together. It features a moist lemon cake generously studded with raspberries and topped with lemon and raspberry buttercream icing. Serve it with fresh raspberries and a glass of cold milk for the perfect afternoon pick-me-up!
Servings: Serves 12
Preparation Time: 20 minutes
Ready Time: 1 hour

Ingredients:
- 2 1/4 cups all-purpose flour
- 2 tsp baking powder
- 1/2 tsp baking soda

- 1/2 tsp salt
- 1/2 cup (1 stick) butter, softened
- 1 1/2 cups sugar
- 2 large eggs
- 1/2 cup buttermilk
- 2/3 cup fresh lemon juice
- 2 tsp lemon zest
- 1 cup fresh raspberries, divided
- 3/4 cup heavy cream

Instructions:
1. Preheat your oven to 350°F. Grease and flour two nine-inch round cake pans and set aside.
2. In a medium bowl, whisk together the flour, baking powder, baking soda, and salt.
3. In a separate bowl, cream together the butter and sugar until light and fluffy. Add the eggs one at a time, and mix until incorporated.
4. In a third bowl, mix together the buttermilk, lemon juice and lemon zest.
5. Slowly add the dry Ingredients to the butter mixture, alternating with the buttermilk mixture. Beat until fully incorporated.
6. Gently fold in 3/4 cup of the raspberries.
7. Divide the batter between the two cake pans, and bake for 25-30 minutes, or until a toothpick inserted in the center comes out clean.
8. Allow to cool for 10 minutes in the pan before transferring to a cooling rack to cool completely.
9. Once the cake is cool, assemble the cake using the remaining raspberries and the heavy cream.

Nutrition Information: Per Serving: 542 Calories, 24g Fat, 70g Carbohydrates, 6g Protein, 10g Fiber

7. lemon poppy seed cake

Lemon Poppy Seed Cake - A flavorful, zesty, and moist cake made with poppy seeds and lemon flavor, this lemon poppy seed cake is sure to be a hit with family and friends!
Serving: 10

Preparation Time: 10 minutes
Ready Time: 1 hour

Ingredients:
- 3 cups all-purpose flour
- 2 teaspoons baking powder
- 1/2 teaspoon salt
- 2 cups white sugar
- 1 cup butter, room temperature
- 4 eggs
- 1 cup milk
- 1 teaspoon vanilla extract
- 2 tablespoons poppy seeds
- 1/3 cup freshly squeezed lemon juice
- 2 tablespoons grated lemon zest

Instructions:
1. Preheat the oven to 350°F (175°C). Grease and flour a 9x13-inch baking pan.
2. In a medium bowl, whisk together the flour, baking powder, and salt.
3. In a large bowl, cream together the sugar and butter until light and fluffy. Add the eggs one at a time, beating well after each addition.
4. Gradually add the dry Ingredients to the creamed mixture alternately with the milk. Beat in the vanilla extract. Stir in the poppy seeds.
5. Pour the batter into the prepared pan.
6. Drizzle the lemon juice over the batter, and sprinkle with the lemon zest.
7. Bake for 35-40 minutes, or until a toothpick inserted into the center of the cake comes out clean.
8. Allow the cake to cool in the pan before serving.

Nutrition Information:
Calories: 390; Total Fat: 17.4g; Saturated Fat: 10.1g; Cholesterol: 107mg; Sodium: 230mg; Total Carbohydrates: 51.6g; Dietary Fiber: 1.2g; Sugars: 33.9g; Protein: 4.9g

8. lemon chiffon cake

Lemon Chiffon Cake is a deliciously light and airy dessert, made with a chiffon cake base that is infused with a bright and zesty lemon flavor. It's the perfect dessert for a special occasion, or when you're craving something sweet and sunny!

Serving: 8 slices
Preparation Time: 15 minutes
Ready Time: 1 hour 10 minutes

Ingredients:
- 2 ½ cups all-purpose flour
- 4 teaspoons baking powder
- ½ teaspoon salt
- ⅔ cup vegetable oil
- 1 ¼ cups granulated sugar
- 8 large eggs (separated)
- ½ teaspoon cream of tartar
- 1 teaspoon vanilla extract
- ½ cup freshly squeezed lemon juice
- ¼ cup whole milk
- Zest of 3 lemons
- Powdered sugar (for dusting)

Instructions:
1. Preheat oven to 350°F (177°C). Grease and flour a 10-inch (25cm) tube pan.
2. In a medium bowl, combine the flour, baking powder, and salt.
3. In the bowl of a stand mixer fitted with the whisk attachment, beat egg whites until foamy. Add cream of tartar and whip until soft peaks form.
4. In a separate large bowl, beat oil and sugar until light and fluffy. Add egg yolks and beat until combined.
5. Add the flour mixture and the milk to the egg/sugar mixture, alternating between the two.
6. Add the vanilla extract, lemon juice, and zest.
7. Carefully fold in the whipped egg whites until just combined.
8. Pour the batter into the prepared pan and bake for 50-60 minutes. Insert a toothpick to the center – it should come out clean.
9. Let the cake cool and dust with powdered sugar before serving.

Nutrition Information: Per serving: Calories: 212, Total fat: 8.7g, Saturated fat: 1.3g, Cholesterol: 97mg, Sodium: 173mg, Total carbs: 30g, Fiber: 0.5g, Sugars: 16.4g, Protein: 5.5g

9. lemon sponge cake

This Lemon Sponge Cake is buttery, moist, and full of zesty lemon flavor! With its simple Ingredients and easy Instructions, it's the perfect cake for special occasions and gatherings.
Serving: Yields 12 slices
Preparation Time: 15 minutes
Ready Time: 1 hour

Ingredients:
- 2 cups all-purpose flour
- 2 teaspoon baking powder
- ½ teaspoon baking soda
- ¼ teaspoon salt
- 2 sticks (1 cup) unsalted butter, softened
- 1 and ½ cup granulated sugar
- 3 large eggs
- 1 teaspoon pure vanilla extract
- ⅔ cup buttermilk
- Zest of 1 lemon
- 2 Tablespoons fresh lemon juice
- 2 tablespoons turbinado sugar

Instructions:
1. Preheat oven to 350°F (177°C). Butter and flour a 9 inch round cake pan.
2. In a small bowl, whisk together flour, baking powder, baking soda, and salt.
3. In a large bowl, beat butter and sugar with an electric mixer until light and fluffy. Add eggs, vanilla, buttermilk, lemon zest, and lemon juice, and beat until combined.
4. Slowly add the dry Ingredients to the wet Ingredients and beat until well blended.

5. Pour the batter into the prepared cake pan and sprinkle with the turbinado sugar.
6. Bake for 35-45 minutes or until a toothpick inserted in the center comes out clean.
7. Let cool in the pan for 15 minutes, then turn out onto a rack and cool completely.

Nutrition Information:
Calories: 204 kcal, Carbohydrates: 28g, Protein: 3g, Fat: 9g, Saturated Fat: 5g, Trans Fat: 0g, Cholesterol: 51mg, Sodium: 174mg, Potassium: 63mg, Fiber: 1g, Sugar: 15g, Vitamin A: 273IU, Vitamin C: 3mg, Calcium: 44mg, Iron: 1mg

10. lemon meringue cake

Lemon Meringue Cake
Serving: 8
Preparation Time: 15 minutes
Ready Time: 45 minutes

Ingredients:
- 4 teaspoons cornstarch
- 1 cup granulated sugar
- ¾ cup water
- 2 tablespoons lemon zest
- 2 tablespoons fresh lemon juice
- 3 egg yolks
- 2 tablespoons butter
- 2 (9-inch) round store-bought shortbread crusts
- 2 egg whites
- 2 tablespoons granulated sugar

Instructions:
1. Preheat the oven to 375°F.
2. In a medium saucepan, mix the cornstarch, sugar, and water over medium heat until it thickens, about 25 minutes.
3. Add the zest, juice, and egg yolks and simmer for 5 minutes.
4. Remove the pan from the heat and stir in the butter.

5. Place one of the shortbread crusts in a 9-inch baking dish and pour the mixture over the crust.
6. Add the remaining crust on top and bake for 20 minutes.
7. Meanwhile, make the meringue by beating the egg whites and sugar until they form stiff peaks.
8. Spread the meringue over the top and bake for 15 to 20 minutes, or until the top is lightly browned.
9. Remove from the oven and let cool before serving.

Nutrition Information:
Calories: 204, Fat: 8g, Cholesterol: 81mg, Sodium: 144mg, Total Carbohydrates: 30g, Fiber: 1g, Sugar: 15g, Protein: 3g.

11. lemon cream cheese cake

Lemon Cream Cheese Cake
Serving: 8
Preparation time: 20 minutes
Ready time: 1 hour 10 minutes

Ingredients:
- 8 ounces cream cheese, softened
- 2 tablespoons lemon zest
- ½ cup butter, softened
- 1 ½ cups sugar
- 2 large eggs
- 1 teaspoon vanilla extract
- 1 ½ cups all-purpose flour
- ¼ teaspoon baking powder
- ¼ teaspoon baking soda
- ¼ teaspoon salt
- ⅔ cup sour cream

Instructions:
1. Preheat oven to 350 degrees Fahrenheit. Grease a 9-inch round cake pan and line the bottom with parchment paper.
2. In a mixing bowl, cream together cream cheese, lemon zest, butter, and sugar until light and fluffy.

3. Beat in eggs, one at a time, and then add vanilla extract.
4. In another bowl, mix together flour, baking powder, baking soda, and salt.
5. Gradually add the dry Ingredients to the wet Ingredients, and mix until just combined.
6. Fold in the sour cream and mix until just combined.
7. Pour the batter into the prepared pan, and smooth out the top.
8. Bake for 45-50 minutes, or until a toothpick inserted into the center comes out clean.
9. Cool the cake in the pan for 10 minutes, and then turn out onto a plate or cake stand and cool completely.

Nutrition Information: Calories 282, Total fat 12g, Saturated fat 7g, Trans fat 0g, Cholesterol 74 mg, Sodium 173 mg, Total carbohydrate 38g, Dietary fiber 0g, Total sugar 22g, Protein 4g.

12. lemon yogurt cake

Lemon Yogurt Cake
Serving: 8
Preparation Time: 10 minutes
Ready Time: 35 minutes

Ingredients:
- 1 3/4 cups all-purpose flour
- 2 teaspoons baking powder
- 3/4 teaspoon baking soda
- 1/2 teaspoon salt
- 3/4 cup plain Greek yogurt
- 2/3 cup granulated sugar
- 1/2 cup vegetable oil
- 2 large eggs
- 1 teaspoon vanilla extract
- 1/4 cup freshly squeezed lemon juice
- 1 teaspoon freshly grated lemon zest
- 2 tablespoons powdered sugar, for dusting

Instructions:

1. Preheat the oven to 350°F. Grease an 8-inch round baking pan.
2. In a medium bowl, whisk together the flour, baking powder, baking soda, and salt.
3. In a large bowl, stir together the yogurt, sugar, oil, eggs, vanilla, lemon juice, and zest until combined.
4. Add the flour mixture to the wet Ingredients in the large bowl and mix until just combined.
5. Pour the batter into the prepared baking pan and bake for 30 to 35 minutes, or until a toothpick inserted into the center of the cake comes out clean.
6. Allow the cake to cool for 10 minutes before turning out onto a serving plate. Dust with powdered sugar before serving.

Nutrition Information:
Per Serving: Calories: 213, Fat: 9g, Saturated fat: 1g, Carbohydrates: 28g, Dietary Fiber: 1g, Protein: 3g, Sodium: 211mg

13. lemon olive oil cake

Lemon Olive Oil Cake is a sweet cake with a light taste of lemon and a hint of the olive oil.
Serving: 8 slices
Preparation Time: 15 minutes
Ready Time: 30 minutes

Ingredients:
-1 cup of all-purpose flour
-3/4 cup of granulated sugar
-1 teaspoon of baking powder
-1/4 teaspoon of salt
-1/3 cup of olive oil
-2 large eggs
-1/2 cup of plus 1 tablespoon of plain yogurt
-Zest of 1 lemon
-1 1/2 tablespoons of fresh lemon juice

Instructions:

1. Preheat oven to 350 degrees F and coat a 9 inch cake pan with cooking spray.
2. In a medium bowl, mix together the flour, sugar, baking powder, and salt.
3. In a separate medium bowl, whisk together the olive oil, eggs, yogurt, lemon zest, and lemon juice until combined.
4. Add the wet Ingredients to the dry Ingredients and mix until just combined. Do not over mix.
5. Pour the cake batter into the prepared pan and bake for 25-30 minutes until an inserted toothpick comes out clean.
6. Let cool before serving.

Nutrition Information:
Per serving (1 slice): Calories - 188 calories, Fat - 8.3 g, Saturated Fat - 1.3 g, Carbohydrates - 25.5 g, Protein - 3.2 g, Sodium - 159 mg

14. lemon coconut cake

Lemon Coconut Cake
Serving: 8 servings
Preparation Time: 15 minutes
Ready Time: 45 minutes

Ingredients:
- 2 1/4 cups all-purpose flour
- 2 teaspoons baking powder
- 1/2 teaspoon baking soda
- 1/2 teaspoon salt
- 1 cup unsalted butter, at room temperature
- 2 cups granulated sugar
- 4 large eggs
- 2 teaspoons vanilla extract
- 3/4 cup coconut milk
- 1/2 cup plain Greek yogurt
- Zest of 2 lemons
- 3 tablespoons freshly squeezed lemon juice
- 2/3 cup sweetened shredded coconut

Instructions:
1. Preheat oven to 350 degrees F. Grease a 9×13 inch baking pan with butter and set aside.
2. In a medium bowl, whisk together the flour, baking powder, baking soda, and salt.
3. In a large bowl, beat the butter and sugar until light and fluffy. Add the eggs one at a time, beating well after each addition. Add the vanilla, coconut milk, yogurt, lemon zest and juice, and mix until combined.
4. Gradually add the dry Ingredients to the wet Ingredients and mix until just combined. Fold in the shredded coconut.
5. Pour the batter into the prepared pan and spread evenly. Bake for 35-40 minutes, or until a toothpick inserted in the center comes out clean.
6. Allow the cake to cool completely before serving.

Nutrition Information:
Calories: 421 kcal, Carbohydrates: 50 g, Protein: 7 g, Fat: 22 g, Saturated Fat: 14 g, Cholesterol: 101 mg, Sodium: 213 mg, Potassium: 80 mg, Fiber: 1 g, Sugar: 28 g, Vitamin A: 704 IU, Vitamin C: 3 mg, Calcium: 77 mg, Iron: 2 mg

15. lemon honey cake

Lemon Honey Cake – A zesty, moist and delicious cake perfect for any occasion!
Serving: 8
Preparation Time: 15 minutes
Ready Time: 45 minutes

Ingredients:
- 3 eggs
- 1 ½ cups all-purpose flour
- 1 teaspoon baking powder
- ¾ cup honey
- 2/3 cup vegetable oil
- ½ teaspoon salt
- 2 tablespoons lemon zest, freshly grated
- 2 tablespoons fresh lemon juice
- 2/3 cup plain yogurt

- 2 teaspoons vanilla extract

Instructions:
1. Preheat the oven to 350°F and lightly grease an 8-inch cake pan.
2. In a large bowl, whisk together the eggs, flour, baking powder, honey, oil, salt, lemon zest, lemon juice, yogurt, and vanilla extract until combined.
3. Pour the batter into the prepared cake pan and bake for about 35-40 minutes, or until a skewer inserted into the center of the cake comes out clean.
4. Allow the cake to cool in the pan for 10 minutes before removing to cool completely on a wire cooling rack.

Nutrition Information:
Calories: 187 kcal, Carbohydrates: 19 g, Protein: 3 g, Fat: 12 g, Saturated Fat: 7 g, Trans Fat: 0.3 g, Cholesterol: 44 mg, Sodium: 125 mg, Potassium: 60 mg, Fiber: 0.4 g, Sugar: 12 g, Vitamin A: 80 IU, Vitamin C: 3.3 mg, Calcium: 30 mg, Iron: 0.7 mg

16. lemon ginger cake

Lemon ginger cake is the perfect balance of sweet and zesty, with the subtle warmth of ginger. Perfect for any occasion, this cake is sure to impress your guests.
Serving: 8
Preparation time: 30 minutes
Ready time: 1 hour

Ingredients:
-1 stick (1/2 cup) butter, softened
-1/2 cup white sugar
-1/2 cup brown sugar
-2 eggs
-1 teaspoon vanilla extract
-2 tablespoons freshly grated lemon zest
-2 teaspoons freshly grated ginger
-1 cup all-purpose flour
-1/2 teaspoon baking soda

- 1/2 teaspoon baking powder
- 1/4 teaspoon salt
- 1/2 cup buttermilk

Instructions:
1. Preheat the oven to 350F.
2. In a medium bowl, cream together the butter and sugars with an electric mixer until light and fluffy. Beat in the eggs one at a time. Stir in the vanilla, lemon zest, and ginger.
3. In a separate bowl, whisk together the flour, baking soda, baking powder, and salt.
4. Gradually add the dry Ingredients to the wet Ingredients and mix until just combined.
5. Stir in the buttermilk until mixture is smooth.
6. Pour the batter into a greased 9-inch round cake pan and bake for 35-40 minutes, or until the cake is golden brown and a toothpick inserted into the center comes out clean.
7. Let the cake cool in the pan for 10 minutes and then carefully remove it from the pan and transfer it to a wire rack to cool completely.

Nutrition Information:
Calories: 266 kcal, Carbohydrates: 35 g, Protein: 3.3 g, Fat: 13.9 g, Cholesterol: 55 mg, Sodium: 206 mg, Potassium: 54 mg, Fiber: 0.6 g, Sugar: 21 g, Vitamin A: 464 IU, Calcium: 30 mg, Iron: 1 mg

17. lemon lavender cake

Lemon lavender cake is a light and delicate cake that is perfect for any special occasion. Its distinct combination of flavors makes it a truly delightful treat!
Servings: 12
Preparation Time: 15 minutes
Ready Time: 1 hour

Ingredients:
- 2 cups all-purpose flour
- 1 teaspoon baking powder
- ½ teaspoon baking soda

- ½ teaspoon salt
- 1/3 cup softened butter
- 1 cup white sugar
- 2 eggs
- ¾ cup milk
- Zest of 1 lemon
- Juice from 1 fresh lemon
- 2 teaspoons lavender extract

Instructions:
1. Preheat the oven to 350 degrees F. Grease a 9-inch round cake pan.
2. In a bowl, whisk together the flour, baking powder, baking soda, and salt.
3. In another bowl, cream together the butter and sugar until light and fluffy. Beat in the eggs one at a time, then mix in the milk, lemon zest, lemon juice, and lavender extract.
4. Gradually add the dry Ingredients to the wet and mix until just combined.
5. Pour the batter into the prepared pan and bake for 30-35 minutes, or until a toothpick comes out clean from the center.
6. Let cool before serving.

Nutrition Information (per serving):
Calories: 300; Total Fat: 10g; Saturated Fat: 6g; Cholesterol: 65mg; Sodium: 200mg; Total Carbohydrates: 48g; Dietary Fiber: 1g; Sugars: 28g; Protein: 4g.

18. strawberry lemon cake

Strawberry Lemon Cake: This moist and delicious strawberry lemon cake is the perfect treat to enjoy any time of the year. Perfectly blending the sweet taste of ripe strawberries with the tartness of lemon, it's sure to become a favorite dessert for all.
Serving: 8
Preparation Time: 30 minutes
Ready Time: 1 hour

Ingredients:

- ¾ Cup softened butter
- 2 ½ Cups all-purpose flour
- 2 teaspoons baking powder
- ½ teaspoon baking soda
- ¼ teaspoon salt
- 2 Cups granulated sugar
- 4 large eggs
- 4 Tablespoons freshly squeezed lemon juice
- 1 Tablespoon grated lemon zest
- 1 teaspoon vanilla extract
- 1 Cup sour cream
- 2 ½ Cups diced fresh strawberries
- 1 container prepared frosting (can be homemade or store-bought)

Instructions:
1. Preheat the oven to 350 degrees F. Grease and flour two round 8-inch cake pans.
2. In a medium bowl, whisk together the flour, baking powder, baking soda and salt. Set aside.
3. Cream together the butter and sugar until light and fluffy. Add the eggs one at a time, beating well after each addition. Add the lemon juice, zest and vanilla extract, mix until combined.
4. Add the flour mixture to the wet Ingredients in three additions, alternating with the sour cream. Mix until combined.
5. Fold in the diced strawberries.
6. Divide the batter between the two cake pans and bake for 35- 40 minutes, or until a toothpick inserted into the center comes out clean.
7. Allow the cakes to cool in the pan for 10 minutes before transferring to a wire rack to cool completely.
8. Once cooled, use frosting to assemble the cake.

Nutrition Information (for 1 serving):
Calories: 553
Total Fat: 19g
Carbohydrates: 90g
Protein: 6g
Sodium: 286mg
Sugar: 58g

19. lemon rose cake

Lemon Rose Cake
Serving: 8
Preparation time: 20 minutes
Ready time: 1 hour

Ingredients:
- 2 cups of all-purpose flour
- 2 teaspoons of baking powder
- ¼ teaspoon of salt
- 1 cup of unsalted butter, softened
- 1 ½ cups of granulated sugar
- 3 eggs
- 1 tablespoon of lemon zest
- 1 teaspoon of rosewater
- ¾ cup of buttermilk
- 2 tablespoons of dried rose petals for garnish

Instructions:
1. Preheat oven to 350°F (180°C), and grease and line an 8-inch round cake tin.
2. In a medium bowl, sift together the flour, baking powder, and salt.
3. In a large bowl, mix together the butter and sugar until light and fluffy.
4. Beat in the eggs one at a time, stirring in the lemon zest along with the last egg.
5. Add the rosewater, and stir until well blended.
6. Add the flour mixture to the butter mixture in two batches, alternating with the buttermilk. Stir until just combined.
7. Pour cake batter into the prepared cake tin, and sprinkle evenly with rose petals.
8. Bake for 45-55 minutes, until a toothpick inserted into the center of the cake comes out clean.
9. Let cool completely and remove from pan before serving.

Nutrition Information: per serving (1/8 of cake): 393 calories, 191 calories from fat, 21g fat, 12g saturated fat, 93mg cholesterol, 268mg sodium, 48g carbohydrates, 1g fiber, 30g sugar, 5g protein

20. lemon apple cake

Lemon Apple Cake
Serving: 8
Preparation Time: 30 minutes
Ready Time: 1 hour and 30 minutes

Ingredients:
- 2/3 cup butter, softened
- 2 cups granulated sugar
- 2 eggs
- 2 teaspoons vanilla extract
- 3 cups all-purpose flour
- 2 teaspoons baking powder
- ¼ teaspoon baking soda
- ½ teaspoon salt
- 1 cup buttermilk
- 2 large apples, peeled, cored, and chopped
- Zest of 2 lemons

Instructions:
1. Preheat your oven to 350°F and lightly grease a 9x13 inch baking pan.
2. In a large bowl, cream together the butter and sugar until light and fluffy. Beat in the eggs one at a time, then add in the vanilla extract.
3. In a separate bowl, whisk together the flour, baking powder, baking soda and salt. Gradually add this dry mixture to the butter mixture, alternating with the buttermilk to create a creamy batter.
4. Fold in the apples and lemon zest.
5. Pour the batter into the greased pan and bake for 40-45 minutes, or until a toothpick inserted in the center of the cake comes out clean.
6. Allow the cake to cool for 10 minutes before cutting and serving.

Nutrition Information:
Serving size: 1 slice
Calories: 276kcal
Total Fat: 11g
Saturated Fat: 7g
Cholesterol: 50mg
Sodium: 163mg
Total Carbohydrates: 40g

Dietary Fiber 2g
Protein: 3g

21. lemon almond cake

Lemon Almond Cake
Serving: 12
Preparation time: 10 minutes
Ready time: 50 minutes

Ingredients:
- 2 cups all-purpose flour
- 2 teaspoons baking powder
- 1/2 teaspoon salt
- 2/3 cup butter, softened
- 2/3 cup white sugar
- 2 eggs
- 1 teaspoon almond extract
- 2/3 cup milk
- 1/2 cup roasted almonds, chopped
- 1/2 cup fresh lemon juice
- 1 tablespoon lemon zest

Instructions:
1. Preheat oven to 350 degrees F (175 degrees C). Grease and flour one 9 inch round cake pan.
2. In a medium bowl, sift together the flour, baking powder and salt.
3. In a large bowl, cream the softened butter and sugar until light and fluffy. Beat in the eggs one at a time. Stir in the almond extract, milk, roasted almonds, lemon juice and lemon zest.
4. Slowly beat in the flour mixture until just incorporated.
5. Pour batter into the prepared pan.
6. Bake in the preheated oven for 40-45 minutes, or until a toothpick inserted into the center of the cake comes out clean. Cool cake on a wire rack for 10 minutes before serving.

Nutrition Information:

Calories: 153kcal Carbohydrates: 13.5g Fat: 9.3g Protein: 2.8g Sodium: 137mg Potassium: 63mg Fiber: 0.7g Sugar: 6.3g Calcium: 30mg Iron: 0.9mg

22. lemon cardamom cake

This Lemon Cardamom Cake is a delicious and moist cake made with lemon juice, lemon zest, and cardamom. It is so easy to make and a perfect addition to any tea party or afternoon snack.
Serving: 8
Preparation Time: 10 minutes
Ready Time: 1 hour

Ingredients:
- 2 cups all-purpose flour
- 1 teaspoon baking powder
- ½ teaspoon baking soda
- 1 teaspoon ground cardamom
- ½ cup (1 stick) unsalted butter, softened
- 1 cup granulated sugar
- 2 large eggs
- 2 lemons, zested and juiced
- ½ cup buttermilk
- ½ teaspoon vanilla extract

Instructions:
1. Preheat oven to 350 degrees F. Grease and line a 9-inch round cake pan with parchment paper.
2. In a medium bowl, whisk together the flour, baking powder, baking soda, and cardamom.
3. In the bowl of a stand mixer fitted with the paddle attachment, beat the butter and sugar together on medium-high speed until light and fluffy, about 3 minutes.
4. Add the eggs, one at a time, beating well after each addition.
5. Add the lemon zest and juice, buttermilk, and vanilla extract. Beat until combined.
6. Reduce the mixer speed to low and slowly add in the flour mixture until combined.

7. Pour the batter into the prepared pan and bake for 35-40 minutes, or until a toothpick inserted into the center comes out clean.
8. Let the cake cool in the pan for 10 minutes before transferring to a wire rack to cool completely.

Nutrition Information:
Serving Size: 1 slice
Calories: 244
Fat: 11g
Carbohydrates: 31g
Protein: 4.5g
Sugar: 16g

23. lemon thyme cake

Lemon Thyme Cake
Serving: 8
Preparation time: 10 minutes
Ready time: 1 hour

Ingredients:
-2 eggs
-1/2 cup vegetable oil
-1 cup buttermilk
-1/4 cup grated lemon zest
-1 teaspoon fresh thyme leaves
-1 teaspoon baking powder
-3/4 teaspoon of baking soda
-3/4 teaspoon of salt
-1 cup sugar
-2 cups all-purpose flour

Instructions:
1. Preheat oven to 350°F.
2. In a medium size mixing bowl whisk eggs and oil until creamy.
3. In a separate bowl, sift together the baking powder, baking soda, salt, and flour.
4. Add the sugar to the egg and oil mixture, slowly stirring.

5. Alternating, add the dry and wet Ingredients to the egg and oil mixture until everything is just mixed together.
6. Add the freshly grated lemon zest and fresh thyme leaves.
7. Grease an 8" cake pan and pour the cake batter into the pan.
8. Bake in preheated oven, 350°F for 25–30 minutes or until a toothpick inserted in the center comes out clean.

Nutrition Information:
Calories: 250, Total Fat: 10g, Saturated Fat: 6g, Trans Fat: 0.2g, Cholesterol: 49mg, Sodium: 276mg, Carbohydrates: 36g, Dietary Fiber: 1g, Sugar: 20g, Protein: 3g

24. lemon lime cake

Our delicious Lemon-Lime Cake is filled with a refreshing, zesty flavor that is sure to bring a smile to your face!
Serving: 12 people
Preparation Time: 25 minutes
Ready Time: 1 hour

Ingredients:
- 2 1/4 cups all-purpose flour
- 1 teaspoon baking powder
- 1 teaspoon baking soda
- 1/2 cup butter, softened
- 2/3 cup granulated sugar
- 2 eggs
- 1 teaspoon lemon extract
- 1 teaspoon lime extract
- 3/4 cup buttermilk
- Lemon and lime zest for garnish

Instructions:
1. Preheat oven to 350 degrees F. Grease and flour a 9 inch cake pan.
2. In a large bowl, combine the flour, baking powder, and baking soda.
3. In a separate bowl, cream together the butter and sugar until combined. Add the eggs, one at a time, beating in between each addition. Add the lemon and lime extracts.

4. Alternating between the dry Ingredients and buttermilk, add half of each to the wet Ingredients, beating until combined. Once all of the Ingredients are combined, pour into the prepared cake pan. Bake in the preheated oven for 30-35 minutes, or until a toothpick inserted into the center of the cake comes out clean. Allow to cool for 15 minutes before turning out onto a wire cooling rack.

5. Once the cake has cooled completely, use a knife to spread a thin layer of buttercream or cream cheese frosting and sprinkle with lemon and lime zest for garnish.

Nutrition Information:
Serving size: 1 slice
Calories: 250
Fat: 9g
Saturated fat: 5g
Trans fat: 0g
Carbohydrates: 37g
Sugar: 19g
Protein: 4g
Cholesterol: 51mg
Sodium: 234mg

25. lemon banana cake

Lemon Banana Cake:
Serving: 8
Preparation Time: 10 minutes
Ready Time: 45 minutes

Ingredients:
-1/2 cup butter
-1 1/2 cups sugar
-2 eggs
-1 3/4 cups all-purpose flour
-1 teaspoon baking soda
-1 teaspoon baking powder
-1 teaspoon salt
-1 cup mashed bananas

- 1 cup buttermilk
- 1 teaspoon vanilla extract
- 2 tablespoons freshly squeezed lemon juice

Instructions:
1. Preheat the oven to 350 degrees F (175 degrees C). Grease and flour an 8-inch square baking pan.
2. In a medium bowl, cream together the butter and sugar until light and fluffy. Beat in the eggs, one at a time.
3. In a separate bowl, sift together the flour, baking soda, baking powder, and salt. Stir the dry Ingredients into the batter alternately with the mashed bananas and the buttermilk. Beat in the vanilla and lemon juice.
4. Pour the batter into the prepared pan.
5. Bake for 40 to 45 minutes, or until a toothpick inserted into the center of the cake comes out clean.

Nutrition Information:
Calories -338, Fat -14g, Cholesterol -51mg, Sodium -447mg, Carbohydrates -50g, Protein -4g.

26. lemon carrot cake

This zesty Lemon Carrot Cake is a citrusy delight that will make you crave for more. Packed with the goodness of carrots, this cake is likely to become your favorite go-to sweet treat.

Serving: 8
Preparation Time: 25 minutes
Ready Time: 1 hour 30 minutes

Ingredients:
- 3 cups all-purpose flour
- 2 teaspoons baking powder
- 2 teaspoons baking soda
- 1/2 teaspoon salt
- 2 teaspoons ground cinnamon
- 2 cups sugar
- 1 cup vegetable oil
- 4 large eggs

- 2 teaspoons lemon extract
- 2 cups grated carrots
- 2/3 cup chopped walnuts
- 1/2 cup raisins

Instructions:
1. Preheat oven to 350°F. Grease and flour a 9x13 inch baking pan.
2. In a medium bowl, whisk together flour, baking powder, baking soda, salt, and cinnamon.
3. In a large bowl, beat together sugar, oil, eggs, and lemon extract.
4. Gradually mix in the dry Ingredients until just combined.
5. Fold in the carrots, walnuts, and raisins.
6. Spread the batter evenly into the prepared pan.
7. Bake for 45 minutes, or until a toothpick inserted into the center comes out clean.
8. Let cool in the pan for 15 minutes, then turn out onto a wire rack to cool completely.

Nutrition Information: Approximate Calories: 390, Fat: 16 grams, Cholesterol: 55 milligrams, Sodium: 220 milligrams, Carbohydrates: 53 grams, Fiber: 2 grams, Protein: 6 grams.

27. lemon cranberry cake

Lemon Cranberry Cake
Serving: 8-10
Preparation Time: 10 minutes
Ready Time: 1 hour and 30 minutes

Ingredients:
- 2 cups all-purpose flour
- 1 teaspoon baking powder
- 1/4 teaspoon baking soda
- 1/2 teaspoon salt
- 3 tablespoons lemon zest
- 2 sticks butter, room temperature
- 1 cup sugar
- 2 eggs

- 2 teaspoons vanilla extract
- 2/3 cup freshly-squeezed lemon juice
- 1 1/2 cups fresh cranberries
- Powdered sugar, for dusting

Instructions:
1. Preheat oven to 375 F. Grease a 9-inch cake pan and line with parchment paper.
2. In a medium bowl, whisk together the flour, baking powder, baking soda, salt and lemon zest. In a separate bowl, use an electric mixer to cream the butter and sugar until light and fluffy.
3. Beat in the eggs, one at a time, followed by the vanilla extract and lemon juice. Gradually add the dry Ingredients to the wet Ingredients and mix just until everything is combined.
4. Carefully fold in the cranberries and spread the batter into the prepared pan.
5. Bake for 45-50 minutes, or until a toothpick inserted in the center of the cake comes out clean. Cool the cake completely before dusting with powdered sugar.

Nutrition Information:
Calories: 305, Fat: 14g, Cholesterol: 55mg, Sodium: 310mg, Carbohydrates: 39g, Fiber: 1g, Protein: 3g

28. lemon apricot cake

Lemon Apricot Cake
This light and fluffy lemon apricot cake is a delicious dessert for any occasion. It has an impeccable balance of sweet, tart, and tangy flavors that will surely make your taste buds happy. It's easy to make and your family will love it!
Serving: 10
Preparation Time: 20 minutes
Ready In: 1 hour

Ingredients:
- 2 cups all-purpose flour
- 2 teaspoons baking powder

- 1/2 teaspoon baking soda
- 1/2 teaspoon salt
- 2 tablespoons lemon zest
- 1/2 cup (1 stick) butter, melted
- 1 cup white sugar
- 2 eggs
- 1 cup apricot nectar
- 1/2 cup freshly squeezed lemon juice

Instructions:
1. Preheat oven to 350 degrees F (175 degrees C). Grease and flour a 9-inch round baking pan.
2. In a medium bowl, whisk together flour, baking powder, baking soda, salt and lemon zest.
3. In a large bowl, cream together the melted butter and sugar. Beat in the eggs, one at a time.
4. Gradually stir in the flour mixture, alternating with the apricot nectar and lemon juice. Mix until all Ingredients are incorporated.
5. Pour the batter into the prepared pan.
6. Bake for 30 to 40 minutes in the preheated oven, or until a toothpick inserted into the center of the cake comes out clean.
7. Allow to cool before serving.

Nutrition Facts:
- Serving Size: 1 slice
- Calories: 227
- Carbs: 33g
- Protein: 2g
- Fat: 9.3g
- Saturated Fat: 5.5g
- Cholesterol: 54mg
- Sodium: 135mg
- Potassium: 121mg
- Fiber: 1g
- Sugar: 16g
- Vitamin A: 295 IU
- Vitamin C: 3.5mg
- Calcium: 54mg
- Iron: 1mg

29. lemon fig cake

Enjoy the sweetness of figs and the tartness of lemon in this moist and flavorful lemon fig cake!
Serving: 8
Preparation Time: 20 minutes
Ready Time: 2 hours

Ingredients:
- 3/4 cup all-purpose flour
- 1 teaspoon baking powder
- 1/4 teaspoon baking soda
- 1/4 teaspoon salt
- 3 large eggs
- 3/4 cup white sugar
- 1 teaspoon vanilla extract
- 1/2 cup unsalted butter, melted
- 1/2 cup low-fat plain yogurt
- 1 tablespoon finely grated lemon zest
- 2 tablespoons freshly squeezed lemon juice
- 1 cup finely chopped fresh or dried figs

Instructions:
1. Preheat the oven to 350°F. Grease and flour a 9-inch round cake pan, set aside.
2. In a medium bowl, whisk together the flour, baking powder, baking soda, and salt.
3. In a large bowl, using an electric mixer, beat the eggs and sugar on medium-high speed until light and fluffy.
4. Beat in the vanilla extract, butter, yogurt, lemon zest, and lemon juice.
5. Slowly add the dry Ingredients to the wet Ingredients. Mix until just combined.
6. Fold in the figs.
7. Transfer the batter to the prepared cake pan.
8. Bake for 35-40 minutes, or until a toothpick inserted into the center comes out clean.
9. Let cool in the pan for 15 minutes before transferring to a wire rack.
10. Let cool completely before slicing and serving.

Nutrition Information:

Calories: 250, Total Fat: 10 g, Sodium: 130 mg, Potassium: 90 mg, Carbohydrates: 32 g, Dietary Fiber: 1 g, Protein: 4 g, Vitamin A: 7%, Vitamin C: 5%, Calcium: 5%, Iron: 5%

30. lemon hazelnut cake

Lemon Hazelnut Cake
Serving: 8 slices
Preparation time: 30 minutes
Ready time: 1 hour and 30 minutes

Ingredients:
- 2 ½ cups all-purpose flour
- 2 teaspoons baking powder
- ½ teaspoon baking soda
- ¼ teaspoon salt
- 2/3 cup vegetable oil
- 1 cup granulated sugar
- 1/3 cup chopped hazelnuts
- 2 large eggs
- 1 teaspoon vanilla extract
- ¾ cup buttermilk
- 1 tablespoon grated lemon zest
- 2 tablespoons fresh lemon juice

Instructions:
1. Preheat oven to 350°F (177°C). Grease an 8-inch round cake pan.
2. In a medium bowl, whisk together the flour, baking powder, baking soda, and salt; set aside.
3. In a separate bowl, whisk together the oil, sugar, and hazelnuts. Then add the eggs, vanilla extract, and buttermilk and mix until fully blended.
4. Add the dry Ingredients and stir until combined.
5. Fold in the lemon zest and the lemon juice.
6. Pour batter into the prepared baking pan.
7. Bake in pre-heated oven for 30 minutes, or until a tester inserted in the middle comes out clean.
8. Allow the cake to cool completely before serving.

Nutrition Information:
Per 1 slice (1/8th of cake): Calories: 325; Fat: 17.3g; Carbs: 38.2g; Protein: 4.1g.

31. lemon peach cake

This tart and sweet Lemon Peach Cake is the perfect summer dessert. It's easy to make and takes advantage of seasonal peaches and lemons for an irresistible balance of flavor.
Serving: 8-10 slices
Preparation Time: 10 minutes
Ready Time: 1 hour

Ingredients:
- 2 cups all-purpose flour
- 2 teaspoons baking powder
- 1/2 teaspoon fine salt
- 1 cup softened butter
- 1 cup white sugar
- 2 eggs
- 1 teaspoon almond extract
- 4 tablespoons freshly squeezed lemon juice
- 3 ripe peaches, peeled and chopped

Instructions:
1. Preheat oven to 350°F / 180°C. Grease and flour a 9-inch cake pan.
2. In a medium bowl, mix together flour, baking powder and salt.
3. In a separate bowl, cream together butter and sugar until light and fluffy. Beat in eggs, one at a time, then stir in almond extract and lemon juice, mixing until well blended.
4. Gradually stir in flour mixture.
5. Spread batter evenly into the cake pan.
6. Arrange peach slices on top of the batter in an even pattern.
7. Bake for 40 minutes or until a toothpick inserted into the center of the cake comes out clean.

Nutrition Information:

Calories: 282, Fat: 14.9 g, Cholesterol: 60 mg, Sodium: 187 mg, Carbohydrates: 37.1 g, Fiber: 1.7 g, Protein: 3.2 g.

32. lemon pistachio cake

Lemon Pistachio Cake
Serving: 8 slices
Preparation Time: 25 minutes
Ready Time: 1 hour

Ingredients:
- 2 cups granulated sugar
- 1 1/4 cups all-purpose flour
- 3 large eggs
- 1/2 teaspoon salt
- 1/3 cup melted butter
- 1 teaspoon baking powder
- 1 cup milk
- 2 tablespoons fresh lemon juice
- 2 teaspoons lemon zest
- 2 tablespoons finely chopped pistachios

Instructions:
1. Preheat the oven to 350°F. Grease and flour a 9-inch round cake pan.
2. In a medium bowl, whisk together the sugar and flour.
3. In a large bowl, beat the eggs until light and fluffy. Add the melted butter and mix until fully incorporated.
4. Add the sugar and flour mixture to the egg mixture and beat until combined.
5. Add the salt, baking powder, milk, lemon juice, and lemon zest and mix until everything is incorporated.
6. Pour the batter into the prepared cake pan and sprinkle the chopped pistachios on top.
7. Bake the cake for 35-40 minutes or until a toothpick inserted into the center comes out clean.
8. Let the cake cool for 10 minutes before turning out onto a wire rack to cool completely.

Nutrition Information (per slice): Calories: 327, Fat: 11.6 g, Saturated Fat: 6.8 g, Cholesterol: 68.5 mg, Carbohydrates: 49.2 g, Sugar: 16.6 g, Protein: 8.2 g, Fiber: 0.1 g

33. lemon plum cake

This delicious Lemon Plum Cake has the perfect amount of tart and sweet flavors combined with a moist crumb. It's perfect for a Sunday brunch or an afternoon coffee break.
Serving: 12
Preparation Time: 15 minutes
Ready Time: 45 minutes

Ingredients:
- 2 cups all-purpose flour
- 1 teaspoon baking powder
- 1 teaspoon baking soda
- ½ teaspoon of salt
- ¾ cup white sugar
- ½ cup butter, softened
- 2 large eggs, at room temperature
- 2 tablespoons freshly squeezed lemon juice
- 1 teaspoon vanilla extract
- 3 plums, peeled and sliced thinly
- 1 tablespoon butter
- 1 tablespoon granulated sugar

Instructions:
1. Preheat oven to 350°F (175°C). Grease a 9-inch round cake pan and set aside.
2. In a medium bowl, whisk together flour, baking powder, baking soda, and salt.
3. In a separate large bowl, cream together butter and sugar until light and fluffy. Beat in the eggs, one at a time.
4. Add the flour mixture to the butter mixture and stir to combine.
5. Beat in the lemon juice and vanilla extract until well combined.
6. Spread batter evenly in the prepared cake pan.
7. Top with plum slices and sprinkle with the remaining butter and sugar.

8. Bake for 35-45 minutes or until the top is golden and a toothpick inserted into the center comes out clean.
9. Let cool for 10 minutes before removing from the cake pan.

Nutrition Information per Serving: Calories: 258 kcal, Carbohydrates: 32 g, Protein: 4 g, Fat: 12 g, Saturated Fat: 7 g, Cholesterol: 58 mg, Sodium: 212 mg, Potassium: 77 mg, Fiber: 1 g, Sugar: 17 g, Vitamin A: 400 IU, Vitamin C: 4.3 mg, Calcium: 34 mg, Iron: 1.2 mg

34. lemon rum cake

Lemon Rum Cake is a moist, fluffy cake full of flavor and a hint of lemon zest. Serve it as a dessert to friends or at a party for a delicious treat!
Serving: 8-10 slices
Preparation Time: 25 minutes
Ready Time: 1 hour

Ingredients:
- 2 1/2 cups all-purpose flour
- 3 teaspoon baking powder
- 1/2 teaspoon salt
- 1/2 cup butter, softened
- 1/2 cup vegetable oil
- 1 3/4 cups sugar
- 4 large eggs
- 2 teaspoon vanilla extract
- 3/4 cup sour cream
- 1 teaspoon lemon zest
- 1/4 cup dark rum
- 1/4 cup powdered sugar

Instructions:
1. Preheat oven to 350°F (175°C). Grease and flour a 9-inch x 13-inch baking pan.
2. In a medium bowl, whisk together the flour, baking powder and salt.

3. In a large bowl, cream together the butter, oil and 1 1/2 cups sugar until light and fluffy. Beat in the eggs, one at a time, then stir in the vanilla extract, sour cream, lemon zest and rum.
4. Gradually add in the dry Ingredients and mix until combined.
5. Pour batter into the prepared pan and spread evenly. Bake for 35-40 minutes, or until a toothpick inserted into the center comes out clean.
6. In a small bowl, whisk together the remaining sugar and powdered sugar. Sprinkle over the warm cake. Let cool before serving.

Nutrition Information:
Calories: 365; Total Fat: 11.5g; Cholesterol: 90mg; Sodium: 206mg; Total Carbohydrate: 57.3g; Protein: 4.2g

35. lemon sesame cake

This Lemon Sesame Cake is sure to tantalize your taste buds with its delectable blend of sweet and tart flavors. With its moist sponge cake and delightful topping, this dish is a perfect way to finish off any meal!
Serving: 6-8 servings
Preparation Time:
25 minutes
Ready Time:
2 hours

Ingredients:
2 cups all-purpose flour
2 ½ teaspoons baking powder
1 teaspoon salt
3 tablespoons white sugar
1 cup vegetable oil
2 large eggs
¾ cup milk
2 tablespoons lemon zest
1 teaspoon vanilla extract
2 tablespoons sesame seeds

Instructions:

1. Preheat oven to 350°F. Grease a 9-inch round cake pan with oil and line with parchment paper.
2. In a medium mixing bowl, whisk together the flour, baking powder, salt, and sugar.
3. In a separate large bowl, whisk together the oil, eggs, milk, lemon zest, and vanilla extract.
4. Gradually add the dry Ingredients to the wet Ingredients, stirring to combine.
5. Pour the batter into the prepared cake pan and sprinkle the sesame seeds over the top.
6. Bake for 25 minutes or until a toothpick inserted into the centre of the cake comes out clean.
7. Let the cake cool in the pan for 15 minutes before inverting onto a serving plate.

Nutrition Information:
Servings per Recipe: 8
Calories: 320
Fat: 18.4g
Carbohydrates: 32.3g
Protein: 4.2g
Sodium: 222mg
Sugar: 8.8g

36. lemon tea cake

This Lemon Tea Cake is light and flavorful with a hint of citrus and a sweet, buttery glaze. Perfect for any occasion, you'll pleasantly surprise your family and friends with this impressive tea cake.
Serving: 12
Preparation Time: 30 minutes
Ready Time: 1 hour

Ingredients:
- 2 1/2 cups all-purpose flour
- 1 teaspoon baking powder
- 1/2 teaspoon baking soda
- 1/4 teaspoon freshly ground black pepper

- 1/2 teaspoon salt
- 1/2 cup butter, softened
- 1 cup granulated sugar
- 2 large eggs
- 1 1/2 teaspoons lemon zest
- 1/2 cup buttermilk
- 2 tablespoons freshly squeezed lemon juice
- 1 tablespoon grated lemon zest, for garnish

Instructions:
1. Preheat oven to 350°F (175°C). Grease and flour a 8-inch round cake pan and set aside.
2. In a medium bowl, combine flour, baking powder, baking soda, pepper and salt.
3. In a separate bowl, cream together butter and sugar until light and fluffy. Add eggs one at a time, beating well after each addition.
4. Add the dry Ingredients, alternating with the buttermilk and lemon juice. Mix until just combined.
5. Transfer the batter into the prepared pan and bake for 35-40 minutes, until a toothpick inserted into the center comes out clean.
6. Cool the cake for 10 minutes before turning it out onto a serving plate. Garnish with the remaining lemon zest.

Nutrition Information:
Serving size 1 slice (38g)
Calories 167kcal, Fat 4.5g, Cholesterol 25mg, Sodium 131mg, Carbohydrate 28.7g, Protein 2.4g

37. lemon walnut cake

Lemon Walnut Cake
Serving: 12
Preparation time: 15 minutes
Ready time: 1 hour

Ingredients:
- 2 cups of all-purpose flour
- 2 teaspoons baking powder

- 1/2 teaspoon baking soda
- 1/2 teaspoon salt
- 2 sticks unsalted butter, softened
- 1 cup granulated sugar
- 2 large eggs
- 2/3 cups sour cream
- Zest of 2 lemons
- 2 tablespoons freshly squeezed lemon juice
- 1/2 cup chopped walnuts

Instructions:
1. Preheat the oven to 350 degrees F and grease a 9-inch round cake pan.
2. Sift together the flour, baking powder, baking soda, and salt.
3. Cream the butter and sugar together until light and fluffy.
4. Beat in the eggs one at a time.
5. Slowly add the dry Ingredients to the wet Ingredients and mix until combined.
6. Fold in the sour cream, lemon zest, lemon juice, and chopped walnuts.
7. Pour the batter into the prepared pan and bake for 40-45 minutes or until a toothpick inserted into the center of the cake comes out clean.
8. Allow the cake to cool before serving.

Nutrition Information (Per Serving): Calories: 440, Fat: 23g, Saturated Fat: 14g, Trans Fat: 0g, Cholesterol: 78mg, Sodium: 242mg, Carbohydrates: 53g, Fiber: 2g, Sugar: 30g, Protein: 5g

38. blueberry lemon ricotta cake

Indulge in the tantalizing combination of tangy lemons and sweet blueberries in this delicious Blueberry Lemon Ricotta Cake!
Serving: 8
Preparation Time: 20 min
Ready Time: 1 hour

Ingredients:
- ¼ cup (60 g) butter, melted
- 2 cup (250 g) all-purpose flour
- 1 cup (200 g) granulated sugar

- 2 teaspoons baking powder
- ½ teaspoon baking soda
- ¼ teaspoon salt
- 2 eggs, lightly beaten
- 1 cup (245 g) ricotta cheese
- Zest of 1 lemon
- ¼ cup (60 ml) freshly-squeezed lemon juice
- 1 teaspoon pure vanilla extract
- 1 cup (110 g) fresh blueberries

Instructions:
1. Preheat oven to 350F (180C). Grease and flour an 8-inch (20 cm) round cake pan and set aside.
2. In a large bowl, whisk together the flour, sugar, baking powder, baking soda, and salt.
3. In a separate bowl, mix together the melted butter, eggs, ricotta cheese, lemon zest, lemon juice, and vanilla extract.
4. Add the wet Ingredients to the dry Ingredients and mix until just combined. Fold in the blueberries.
5. Pour the batter into the prepared cake pan and bake for 40-45 minutes, or until a toothpick inserted into the center of the cake comes out with just a few moist crumbs.
6. Allow the cake to cool in the pan for 15 minutes, then remove and transfer to a wire cooling rack to cool completely before serving.

Nutrition Information: (per serving)
Calories: 250; Fat: 11g; Saturated Fat: 6g; Cholesterol: 65mg; Sodium: 230mg; Carbohydrates: 33g; Fiber: 1g; Sugar: 16g; Protein: 6g.

39. lemon cherry cake

This delicious lemon cherry cake is moist and has a delicious tartness from the lemon. The cherries add a bit of sweetness and makes it a great dessert to share.
Serving: 8
Preparation Time: 15 minutes
Ready Time: 1 hour

Ingredients:
- 1¾ cups all-purpose flour
- 2 teaspoons baking powder
- ¼ teaspoon salt
- 3/4 cup butter, softened
- 2 cups sugar
- 4 eggs
- 1 teaspoon almond extract
- 1 cup evaporated milk
- 3 tablespoons grated lemon zest
- 1 (21-ounce) can cherry pie filling

Instructions:
1. Preheat oven to 350 °F. Grease and flour a 9x13 inch cake pan.
2. In a medium bowl, mix together the flour, baking powder, and salt.
3. In a large bowl, cream together the butter and sugar until light and fluffy.
4. Add eggs one at a time, mixing well after each addition.
5. Mix in the almond extract, evaporated milk, and lemon zest.
6. Gradually add the flour mixture to the wet Ingredients until everything is well combined.
7. Pour the batter into the prepared cake pan.
8. Spread the cherry pie filling evenly over the top of the cake.
9. Bake for 40-45 minutes, or until a toothpick inserted in the center comes out clean.
10. Let cool before cutting and serving.

Nutrition Information: Calories: 447, Fat: 22g, Total Carbohydrates: 56g, Fiber: 1g, Protein: 6g, Sodium: 00mg, Cholesterol: 77 mg

40. lemon matcha cake

Lemon Matcha Cake
Serving: 8 to 10
Preparation Time: 15 minutes
Ready Time: 1 hour

Ingredients:
- 1 ½ cups all-purpose flour
- 1 teaspoon baking powder
- 2 tablespoons matcha powder
- 1 can (14 oz) condensed milk
- 3 eggs
- ½ cup (1 stick) melted butter
- 2 tablespoons lemon juice
- 2 tablespoons lemon zest

Instructions:
1. Preheat oven to 350°F. Grease an 8-inch cake pan and line with parchment paper.
2. In a medium bowl, whisk together the flour, baking powder, and matcha powder.
3. In a separate bowl, whisk together the condensed milk, eggs, butter, lemon juice, and lemon zest.
4. Slowly add the dry Ingredients to the wet and stir until just combined.
5. Pour the batter into the prepared pan and bake for 30-35 minutes or until cake is golden and a toothpick inserted into the center comes out clean.
6. Cool to room temperature before serving.

Nutrition Information:
Calories: 307kcal | Carbohydrates: 32g | Protein: 6g | Fat: 16g | Saturated Fat: 9g | Trans Fat: 1g | Cholesterol: 85mg | Sodium: 74mg | Potassium: 141mg | Fiber: 1g | Sugar: 20g | Vitamin A: 520IU | Vitamin C: 2.8mg | Calcium: 94mg | Iron: 1.4mg

41. lemon orange cake

Lemon Orange Cake
Serving: 8-10
Preparation Time: 45 minutes
Ready Time: 1 hour 45 minutes

Ingredients:
- 3 large eggs

- 1/2 cup vegetable oil
- 1/2 cup freshly squeezed orange juice
- 2 tsp freshly grated orange zest
- 2 tsp freshly grated lemon zest
- 1/4 cup freshly squeezed lemon juice
- 1 3/4 cup all-purpose flour
- 2 tsp baking powder
- 3/4 tsp salt
- 1/2 cup milk
- 1 1/4 cup sugar
- Powdered sugar for dusting (optional)

Instructions:
1. Preheat oven to 350°F and prepare an 8-inch cake pan.
2. Whisk together the eggs, oil, orange juice, orange zest, lemon zest, and lemon juice in a bowl.
3. Sift together the flour, baking powder, and salt in another bowl.
4. In a separate bowl, mix milk and sugar until the sugar is dissolved.
5. Then add the wet Ingredients to the milk/sugar mixture and stir until mixed.
6. Add the dry Ingredients to the wet Ingredients and mix until combined.
7. Pour the batter into the prepared pan and bake in preheated oven for about 45 minutes.
8. Let cool, sprinkle with powdered sugar if desired, and serve.

Nutrition Information per serving (1 slice):
- Calories: 216
- Fat: 9 g
- Carbohydrates: 30 g
- Protein: 3 g

42. lemon blackberry cake

Lemon blackberry cake is an irresistible spring dessert, combining sweet and tart flavors of the fruit with buttery and soft cake! It's the perfect treat to invite friends or family over for tea.
Serving: 8-10 servings

Preparation Time: 10 minutes
Ready Time: 1 hour

Ingredients:
- 2 cups all-purpose flour
- 1/2 teaspoon baking powder
- 1/2 teaspoon baking soda
- 1 teaspoon salt
- 1/2 cup unsalted butter, softened
- 1 cup white sugar
- 2 eggs
- 2 teaspoons lemon zest
- 1/4 cup fresh lemon juice
- 1 teaspoon pure vanilla extract
- 2/3 cup plain Greek yogurt
- 2 cups fresh blackberries

Instructions:
1. Preheat the oven to 350°F. Grease and flour 9" round cake pan.
2. In a medium bowl, mix together the flour, baking powder, baking soda, and salt. Set aside.
3. Using an electric mixer, beat the butter and sugar until light and creamy.
4. Add in the eggs, one at a time until combined.
5. Add in the lemon zest, lemon juice, and vanilla extract and continue to mix.
6. Slowly add in the dry Ingredients, mixing on low speed until just combined.
7. Gently fold in the yogurt and blackberries and pour the batter into the prepared cake pan.
8. Bake for 45-50 minutes or until a toothpick comes out clean when inserted into the cake.
9. Allow to cool for 10 minutes before removing from pan and then cool completely.

Nutrition Information (per serving): 264 calories; 9g fat; 42g carbohydrates; 4g protein.

43. lemon elderflower cake

Lemon Elderflower Cake
Serving: 10
Preparation Time: 20 minutes
Ready Time: 1 hour and 20 minutes

Ingredients:
- 2 ½ cups all-purpose flour
- 2 teaspoons baking powder
- ½ teaspoon baking soda
- ¼ teaspoon salt
- 8 tablespoons butter, softened
- 1 ¼ cups of granulated sugar
- 3 eggs
- 2 tablespoons of freshly squeezed lemon juice
- 2 tablespoons of honey
- 1 tablespoon of elderflower cordial
- 2 teaspoons of lemon zest
- 1 teaspoon of vanilla extract
- 1 cup of whole milk

Instructions:
1. Preheat oven to 350 degrees. Grease a 9-inch round cake pan with butter and set aside.
2. In a medium bowl, whisk together the flour, baking powder, baking soda and salt.
3. In a separate bowl, cream together the butter and sugar until light and fluffy.
4. Beat in the eggs one at a time, followed by the lemon juice, honey, elderflower cordial, lemon zest and vanilla
5. Alternately add the flour mixture and milk to the egg mixture, starting and ending with the flour mixture.
6. Pour the batter into the prepared cake pan and bake for 40-45 minutes, or until a toothpick inserted into the center comes out clean.
7. Allow the cake to cool in the pan for 10 minutes before transferring to a cooling rack.

Nutrition Information (per serving):
Calories: 250

Fat: 9.8g
Carbohydrates: 37.5g
Protein: 3.5g
Sodium: 126 mg

44. lemon fig and goat cheese cake

Lemon Fig and Goat Cheese Cake
Serving: 10
Preparation Time: 30 minutes
Ready Time: 1 hour

Ingredients:
- 1/2 cup (112 grams) unsalted butter, softened
- 3/4 cup (150 grams) firmly packed light brown sugar
- 2 large eggs
- 2-3 tablespoons freshly squeezed lemon juice
- 2 cups (244 grams) all-purpose flour
- 2 teaspoons baking powder
- 1/4 teaspoon salt
- 1/2 cup (123 grams) milk
- 2 cups (320 grams) diced fresh figs
- 2 tablespoons (15 grams) all-purpose flour
- 6 ounces (170 grams) soft goat cheese, cut into cubes
- 2 tablespoons (30 grams) raw sugar

Instructions:
1. Preheat oven to 350°F (180°C). Grease a 9-inch (23 cm) springform pan and line the bottom with parchment paper.
2. In the bowl of a stand mixer fitted with the paddle attachment, cream the butter and brown sugar until light and fluffy, about 3 minutes. Add the eggs one at a time, scraping down the sides of the bowl. Add the lemon juice and mix until fully incorporated.
3. In another bowl, whisk together the flour, baking powder, and salt. With the mixer on low, add the flour mixture to the butter mixture in three additions, alternating with the milk, beginning and ending with the flour. Mix until just combined.

4. Place the figs in a bowl and sprinkle with the 2 tablespoons (15 grams) of flour. Gently fold the flour into the figs. Gently fold the figs into the cake batter.

5. Transfer the batter to the prepared pan. Sprinkle the goat cheese cubes evenly over the top of the batter. Sprinkle the top with raw sugar, if desired.

6. Bake in preheated oven for 55 to 60 minutes, or until a pick inserted into the center comes out clean. Allow to cool in the pan before removing the sides.

Nutrition Information:
Calories: 318 kcal, Carbohydrates: 43 g, Protein: 6 g, Fat: 14 g, Saturated Fat: 8 g, Cholesterol: 61 mg, Sodium: 174 mg, Potassium: 209 mg, Fiber: 2 g, Sugar: 24 g, Vitamin A: 409 IU, Vitamin C: 4 mg, Calcium: 99 mg, Iron: 2 mg

45. lemon chestnut cake

This delicious and fragrant Lemon Chestnut Cake is perfect for any occasion with its light texture and zesty flavors! An easy and delicious one-bowl recipe, this cake is sure to be a hit for your next gathering!
Serving: This Lemon Chestnut Cake serves 4-6 people.
Preparation Time:
Preparation time is 10 minutes.
Ready Time:
This cake is ready in 1 hour.

Ingredients:
- 3/4 cup all-purpose flour
- 3/4 teaspoon baking powder
- 2 teaspoons ground chestnuts
- 1/4 teaspoon salt
- 3 eggs
- 3/4 cup sugar
- 3 tablespoons olive oil
- 2 tablespoons fresh lemon juice
- Zest of one lemon
- 1/4 teaspoon vanilla extract

Instructions:
1. Preheat oven to 350°F. Grease and flour a 9-inch springform pan.
2. In a medium bowl, whisk together flour, baking powder, ground chestnuts, and salt.
3. In a separate bowl, beat eggs until light and frothy. Gradually add in sugar, oil, lemon juice, lemon zest, and vanilla.
4. Gradually add dry Ingredients to wet Ingredients and mix until just combined.
5. Pour batter into prepared pan.
6. Bake for 30-35 minutes, or until a wooden skewer inserted into the center comes out clean.
7. Cool cake in the pan for 10 minutes before turning onto a cooling rack.

Nutrition Information
Serving Size: 1/6 of recipe
Calories: 289, Fat: 12.3g, Carbs: 39g, Protein: 5.4g

46. lemon sweet potato cake

Lemon Sweet Potato Cake
Serving: 8-10
Preparation Time: 15 minutes
Ready Time: 1 hour 20 minutes

Ingredients:
- 2 cups mashed sweet potato
- 1/2 cup melted butter
- 1/2 cup white sugar
- 1/2 cup brown sugar
- 2 eggs
- 1 teaspoon vanilla extract
- 1/2 cup vegetable oil
- 2 cups all-purpose flour
- 2 teaspoons baking powder
- 1/4 teaspoon baking soda
- 1 lemon, zested

- 1 pinch ground nutmeg

Instructions:
1. Preheat oven to 350 degrees F (175 degrees C). Grease and flour a 9x13 inch pan.
2. In a large bowl, mash sweet potatoes. Stir in butter, white sugar, brown sugar, eggs, vanilla extract, and oil.
3. In a separate bowl, combine flour, baking powder, baking soda, lemon zest, and nutmeg. Stir into sweet potato mixture until blended. Pour cake batter into pan.
4. Bake in preheated oven for 1 hour or until a toothpick inserted into the center of the cake comes out clean.

Nutrition Information:
Calories: 241kcal, Carbohydrates: 31g, Protein: 3g, Fat: 12g, Saturated Fat: 6g, Cholesterol: 43mg, Sodium: 86mg, Potassium: 124mg, Fiber: 1g, Sugar: 17g, Vitamin A: 2450IU, Vitamin C: 6.2mg, Calcium: 44mg, Iron: 1.2mg

47. lemon zucchini cake

For a light and fluffy cake with a hint of citrus, try this delicious Lemon Zucchini Cake. This zucchini-infused cake combines the sweetness of lemon with the moistness of fresh zucchini to create a flavor-packed dessert.

Serving: 8-12
Preparation Time: 15 minutes
Ready Time: 55 minutes

Ingredients:
- 2 cups All-purpose Flour
- 2 teaspoons baking powder
- ½ teaspoon baking soda
- 1 teaspoon ground cinnamon
- ½ teaspoon salt
- ½ cup vegetable oil (canola or corn oil)
- 1 cup granulated sugar
- 2 large eggs

- 1 teaspoon vanilla extract
- 2 cups finely grated zucchini
- 1 teaspoon lemon zest
- 2 tablespoons freshly squeezed lemon juice

Instructions:
1. Preheat your oven to 350°F (177°C) and grease a 9-inch cake pan.
2. In a medium bowl, whisk together the flour, baking powder, baking soda, cinnamon, and salt.
3. In a large bowl, combine the oil, sugar, eggs, and vanilla extract. Beat until light and fluffy.
4. Slowly add the dry Ingredients to the wet Ingredients, stirring until just combined.
5. Add the zucchini, lemon zest, and lemon juice, stirring until just combined.
6. Pour the batter into the prepared cake pan and bake for 45 minutes, or until a toothpick inserted into the center comes out clean.
7. Allow the cake to cool completely before serving.

Nutrition Information (per slice):
Calories: 233, Fat: 9g, Saturated Fat: 1.5g, Sodium: 159mg, Carbohydrates: 34g, Fiber: 1.5g, Protein: 3.3g

48. lemon chocolate cake

This moist and fluffy Lemon Chocolate Cake is sure to be a hit with everyone! The perfect combination of sweet lemony flavor and rich creamy chocolate makes this cake an unforgettable treat.
Serving: 6-8
Preparation time: 25-30 minutes
Ready time: 2 hours

Ingredients:
- 3/4 cup all-purpose flour
- 1/2 cup cocoa powder
- 1/2 teaspoon baking powder
- 1/2 teaspoon baking soda
- 1/4 teaspoon salt

- 1/2 cup melted butter
- 1/2 cup caster sugar
- 1/2 cup light brown sugar
- 2 eggs
- 1/4 cup lemon juice
- 1 teaspoon lemon zest
- 1/2 cup buttermilk
- 1/4 cup semi-sweet chocolate chips

Instructions:
1. Preheat your oven to 350°F and lightly grease a 9-inch round cake tin.
2. In a bowl, sift together the flour, cocoa powder, baking powder, baking soda, and salt.
3. In a separate bowl, mix together the melted butter, both sugars, eggs, lemon juice, and lemon zest until well combined.
4. Add in the flour mixture and buttermilk to the wet Ingredients and mix until a batter forms.
5. Fold in the chocolate chips and pour the mixture into the greased tin.
6. Bake for 25-30 minutes, or until a toothpick inserted into the center of the cake comes out clean.
7. Allow to cool for at least an hour before decorating as desired and serving.

Nutrition Information: Per serving (1/8 of cake): 324 calories; 12.7g fat; 42.9g carbohydrates; 5.4g protein.

49. lemon date cake

Lemon Date Cake
2
Serving: 8
3
Preparation time: 20 minutes
4
Ready time: 1 hour
5

Ingredients:

- 3 ½ cups all-purpose flour
- 2 teaspoons baking powder
- 1 teaspoon baking soda
- ½ teaspoon salt
- 2 sticks (8 ounces) unsalted butter, softened
- 1 ½ cups light brown sugar
- ½ cup granulated sugar
- 3 eggs
- 1 ½ cups buttermilk
- 2 teaspoons vanilla extract
- 1 teaspoon freshly grated lemon zest
- 2 tablespoons freshly squeezed lemon juice
-¾ cup chopped dates
-1/2 cup of walnuts

Instructions:
1. Preheat oven to 350 degrees F. Grease and flour a 9-inch cake pan and set aside.
2. In a medium bowl, whisk together the flour, baking powder, baking soda, and salt.
3. In the bowl of an electric mixer, cream together the butter and sugars until light and fluffy. Add the eggs, one at a time, and beat until thoroughly incorporated.
4. Add the buttermilk, vanilla, lemon zest, and lemon juice and mix until fully blended.
5. Gradually add the dry Ingredients to the wet Ingredients, mixing until just combined.
6. Fold in the dates and walnuts.
7. Pour the batter into the prepared cake pan and bake for 45 to 55 minutes or until a toothpick inserted into the center of the cake comes out clean.
8. Allow cake to cool in the pan for 10 minutes before transferring to a wire rack to cool completely.
9. Serve and enjoy!

Nutrition Information (per serving): Calories: 400; Total Fat: 20g; Saturated Fat: 9g; Trans Fat: 0g; Cholesterol: 95mg; Sodium: 290mg; Carbohydrates: 42g; Fiber: 1g; Sugar: 25g; Protein: 5g.

50. lemon gingerbread cake

Lemon Gingerbread Cake
Serving: 8-10
Preparation Time: 15 minutes
Ready Time: 2 hours

Ingredients:
- 2 cups all-purpose flour
- 2 teaspoons baking powder
- 2 teaspoons ground ginger
- 1 teaspoon ground cinnamon
- ½ teaspoon ground allspice
- ½ teaspoon ground cloves
- ½ teaspoon ground nutmeg
- ½ teaspoon salt
- ½ cup (1 stick) unsalted butter, softened
- 1 cup granulated sugar
- 2 large eggs
- ½ cup molasses
- 1 teaspoon vanilla extract
- ¼ cup whole milk
- 2 tablespoons freshly grated lemon zest
- Juice of 1 lemon

Instructions:
1. Preheat the oven to 350°F. Grease and line a 13-by-9-inch baking pan with parchment paper.
2. In a medium bowl, whisk together the flour, baking powder, ginger, cinnamon, allspice, cloves, nutmeg, and salt.
3. In a large bowl, beat the butter and sugar until light and fluffy, about 3 minutes. Add the eggs, one at a time, beating well after each addition. Beat in the molasses, vanilla, milk, lemon zest and juice.
4. Add the dry Ingredients and stir until just combined.
5. Pour the batter into the prepared baking pan and spread evenly.
6. Bake for 25-30 minutes, or until a toothpick inserted in the center comes out clean.

7. Let the cake cool in the pan for 10 minutes, then invert onto a wire rack and let cool completely.

Nutrition Information:
Calories: 163 per serving, Protein: 2g, Carbs: 29g, Fat: 5g, Sodium: 134mg, Iron: 2% of Daily Value

51. lemon cranberry upside-down cake

This lemon cranberry upside-down cake is a delightfully flavored and decorated cake with a zesty citrus twist!
Serving: Serves 8 to 10
Preparation Time: 15 minutes
Ready Time: 1 hour 15 minutes

Ingredients:
- 1/2 cup (1 stick) unsalted butter, plus 2 tablespoons
- 1/2 cup light brown sugar
- 2 cups cranberries
- 2 tablespoons freshly grated lemon zest
- 2 tablespoons freshly squeezed lemon juice
- 1 1/2 cups all purpose flour
- 1 teaspoon baking powder
- 1/4 teaspoon salt
- 1/2 cup granulated sugar
- 2 large eggs
- 1/2 teaspoon vanilla extract
- 2/3 cup buttermilk

Instructions:
- Preheat oven to 350° F. Grease a 9-inch round cake pan.
- Melt butter in a small saucepan and add the brown sugar. Cook over medium heat until the sugar melts and the mixture is bubbly.
- Pour mixture into the prepared pan and spread evenly over the bottom of the pan. Sprinkle the cranberries over the top.
- In a medium bowl, whisk together the flour, baking powder, and salt.

- In a large bowl, cream together the remaining butter with the sugar. Add the eggs one at a time and mix until well combined. Add the vanilla and the lemon zest and juice.
- Alternately add the dry Ingredients and the buttermilk to the butter mixture. Pour the batter into the pan.
- Bake for 45 to 55 minutes, until the cake is golden brown and a toothpick inserted into the center comes out clean. Cool on a wire rack for 10 minutes before inverting onto a plate.

Nutrition Information: Per serving: 270 calories, 12 g fat, 3 g saturated fat, 60 mg cholesterol, 130 mg sodium, 43 g carbohydrate, 2 g fiber, 26 g sugar, 4 g protein.

52. lemon lavender almond cake

A unique, flavorful and incredibly moist lemon lavender almond cake. The combination of the tart lemon zest with fragrant lavender and crunchy almonds will make your taste buds rejoice with every bite!
Serving: 8
Preparation Time: 10 minutes
Ready Time: 1 hour

Ingredients:
- 2 cups all-purpose flour
- 1 teaspoon baking powder
- 1/2 teaspoon baking soda
- 1/2 teaspoon salt
- 1 cup Greek yoghurt
- 2 large eggs
- 3/4 cup granulated sugar
- 1/4 cup olive oil
- Zest of 2 lemons
- 1 tablespoon dried lavender
- 1/3 cup chopped almonds

Instructions:
1. Preheat oven to 350°F. Grease a 9-inch round cake pan.

2. In a medium bowl, whisk together the flour, baking powder, baking soda, and salt.
3. In a separate bowl, whisk together the yogurt, eggs, sugar, and olive oil until combined.
4. Add the dry Ingredients to the wet Ingredients and mix until just combined.
5. Fold in the lemon zest, lavender, and almonds.
6. Pour the batter into the greased cake pan and bake for 35-40 minutes, or until a toothpick comes out clean.
7. Let the cake cool in the pan before slicing and serving.

Nutrition Information: Per serving (1/8 of the cake): Calories: 243, Total Fat: 10 g, Saturated Fat: 2 g, Cholesterol: 38 mg, Sodium: 220 mg, Potassium: 128 mg, Carbohydrates: 34 g, Fiber: 1 g, Sugar: 18 g, Protein: 5 g.

53. lemon macadamia nut cake

This delicious lemon macadamia nut cake is a perfect summer dessert! A blend of fresh lemons and toasted macadamia nuts, this cake is moist, flavorful, and sure to be a hit with everyone.
Serving: 8
Preparation Time: 20 minutes
Ready Time: 1 hour

Ingredients:
-2 1/2 cups unbleached all-purpose flour
-1 teaspoon baking powder
- 1 teaspoon baking soda
-1/2 teaspoon salt
-1 cup buttermilk
-1/2 cup melted butter
-1 teaspoon vanilla extract
-3/4 cup granulated sugar
-1/2 cup packed light brown sugar
-3 large eggs
-1/4 cup freshly squeezed lemon juice
-1/2 cup toasted macadamia nuts, chopped

Instructions:
1. Preheat the oven to 350°F. Grease and flour a 9-inch round cake pan.
2. In a medium bowl, whisk together the flour, baking powder, baking soda, and salt.
3. In a separate bowl, combine the buttermilk, melted butter, and vanilla.
4. In a large bowl, cream together the granulated sugar and brown sugar until light and fluffy. Add the eggs one at a time, beating well after each addition.
5. Add the buttermilk mixture to the sugar mixture and beat until smooth.
6. Slowly add the flour mixture to the wet Ingredients and mix until just combined.
7. Stir in the lemon juice and macadamia nuts.
8. Pour the batter into the prepared pan and bake for 40-45 minutes, or until a toothpick inserted into the center comes out clean.
9. Allow the cake to cool in the pan for 10 minutes before removing and transferring to a wire rack to cool completely.

Nutrition Information:
Calories: 313; Fat: 13.4g; Carbs: 40.7g; Protein: 4.9g; Sodium: 194mg; Sugar: 28.8g

54. lemon orange almond cake

Lemon Orange Almond Cake
Serving: 8
Preparation Time: 10 minutes
Ready Time: 45 minutes

Ingredients:
- 2 1/4 cup all-purpose flour
- 1 teaspoon baking powder
- 1/4 teaspoon baking soda
- 1/4 teaspoon salt
- 1 cup sugar
- 2 large eggs
- 1/2 cup nondeify butter, melted and slightly cooled

- 1/2 cup plain greek yogurt
- 3 tablespoons fresh lemon juice
- 1 tablespoon grated lemon zest
- 1 tablespoon grated orange zest
- 1/2 cup sliced almonds

Instructions:
1. Preheat oven to 350F degrees. Grease an 8inch round baking pan.
2. In a bowl, whisk together the flour, baking powder, baking soda and salt.
3. In a large bowl, using an electric mixer, beat together the sugar, eggs, butter, yogurt, lemon juice, and lemon and orange zest.
4. Add the dry Ingredients and mix until just combined.
5. Fold in the almonds.
6. Pour the batter into the prepared pan and bake for 40-45 minutes, or until a toothpick inserted in the center comes out clean.
7. Allow the cake to cool completely before serving.

Nutrition Information: Calories 315; Protein 4.5g; Fats 14.5g; Carbs 40.3g; Cholesterol 56mg; Sodium 200.3mg.

55. lemon polenta cake

Lemon Polenta Cake is a delightful and refreshing dessert that combines the tanginess of lemons with the rich texture of polenta. This gluten-free cake is perfect for those who are looking for a delicious treat that's also suitable for a gluten-free diet. With its bright citrus flavor and slightly crunchy texture, this cake is sure to impress your guests. Whether served as a sweet ending to a meal or enjoyed with a cup of tea, this Lemon Polenta Cake is bound to become a favorite in your recipe collection.
Serving: 8-10 servings
Preparation time: 20 minutes
Ready time: 1 hour 30 minutes

Ingredients:
- 1 cup fine polenta (cornmeal)
- 1 cup almond flour
- 1 cup granulated sugar

- 1 teaspoon baking powder
- 1/2 teaspoon salt
- 1/2 cup unsalted butter, melted
- 4 large eggs
- Zest of 2 lemons
- Juice of 2 lemons
- 1/2 cup milk (or almond milk for a dairy-free option)
- Powdered sugar, for dusting (optional)

Instructions:
1. Preheat your oven to 350°F (175°C). Grease a round cake pan (9-inch) and line the bottom with parchment paper.
2. In a large bowl, whisk together the polenta, almond flour, granulated sugar, baking powder, and salt until well combined.
3. In a separate bowl, whisk together the melted butter, eggs, lemon zest, lemon juice, and milk.
4. Gradually pour the wet Ingredients into the dry Ingredients, stirring until just combined. Be careful not to overmix.
5. Pour the batter into the prepared cake pan and smooth the top with a spatula.
6. Bake in the preheated oven for about 40-45 minutes or until a toothpick inserted into the center comes out clean.
7. Once baked, remove the cake from the oven and let it cool in the pan for 10 minutes. Then transfer the cake to a wire rack to cool completely.
8. Dust the cooled cake with powdered sugar, if desired, and serve.

Nutrition Information (per serving):
- Calories: 320
- Total fat: 17g
- Saturated fat: 7g
- Cholesterol: 90mg
- Sodium: 260mg
- Total carbohydrates: 37g
- Dietary fiber: 2g
- Sugars: 19g
- Protein: 6g

Please note that these nutritional values are approximate and may vary depending on the specific Ingredients and brands used.

56. lemon pumpkin cake

This lemon pumpkin cake is light, spongy and immensely flavorful. A perfect marriage of tart lemon and sweet pumpkin flavors, this cake is sure to tantalize the taste buds!
Serving: 10-12
Preparation Time: 25 minutes
Ready Time: 1 hour

Ingredients:
- 2 cups all-purpose flour
- 1 cup granulated sugar
- 1 cup canned pumpkin puree
- 1 teaspoon baking soda
- 1 teaspoon baking powder
- 1/2 teaspoon salt
- 1/2 cup vegetable oil
- 2 eggs
- 1/2 cup freshly squeezed lemon juice
- 1 tablespoon freshly grated lemon zest
- Whipped cream and fresh raspberries for garnish (optional)

Instructions:
1. Preheat oven to 350 degrees F. Grease and flour one 9-inch round cake pan; set aside.
2. In a large bowl, whisk together flour, sugar, baking soda, baking powder, and salt.
3. In a separate smaller bowl, mix together the pumpkin puree, oil, eggs, lemon juice, and zest.
4. Add wet Ingredients to dry Ingredients and stir until completely combined.
5. Pour batter into prepared cake pan and bake for 40-50 minutes, or until a toothpick inserted into the center of the cake comes out clean.
6. Remove from oven and allow to cool for 15 minutes before flipping cake out onto a cooling rack.
7. Place cake on a plate or platter and serve with whipped cream and fresh raspberries. Enjoy!

Nutrition Information: Per serving (1/12 of cake): 329 calories, 15 g fat, 43 g carbohydrates, 3 g fiber, 5.5 g protein

57. lemon semolina cake

Lemon Semolina Cake
Serving: 8
Preparation Time: 30 minutes
Ready Time: 1 hour and 30 minutes

Ingredients:
- 2 cups of semolina
- 1 cup of sugar
- 2 eggs
- 2 sticks of butter
- 2 teaspoons of baking powder
- ⅔ cup of freshly squeezed lemon juice
- 2 tablespoons of grated lemon zest

Instructions:
1. Preheat the oven to 350°F.
2. In a large bowl, add the semolina, sugar, and baking powder and mix until combined.
3. In a separate bowl, beat the eggs until soft peaks form.
4. Add the butter to the semolina mixture and mix until combined.
5. Beat the egg mixture into the semolina mixture.
6. Gently fold in the lemon juice and zest.
7. Grease a 9-inch cake pan with butter and pour the mixture into it.
8. Bake for 50-60 minutes, or until a toothpick inserted into the center comes out clean.

Nutrition Information:
Calories: 360, Fat: 13 g, Protein: 6 g, Carbohydrates: 53 g, Sugar: 25 g, Sodium: 147 mg, Fiber: 2 g.

58. lemon strawberry shortcake

Lemon Strawberry Shortcake
Serving: 4

Preparation Time: 10 minutes
Ready Time: 45 minutes

Ingredients:
- 2 cups all-purpose flour
- 2 teaspoons baking powder
- 1 teaspoon kosher salt
- 6 tablespoons cold unsalted butter, cut into cubes
- 3 tablespoons sugar
- Zest of 1 lemon
- 1 cup heavy cream
- 1 cup fresh strawberries, sliced
- 2 tablespoons sugar
- 4 tablespoons unsalted butter, melted
- 3 tablespoons freshly squeezed lemon juice

Instructions:
1. Preheat oven to 350 degrees F.
2. In a large bowl, combine flour, baking powder, salt, butter, sugar, and lemon zest. Mix with a pastry blender or your hands until it resembles small peas.
3. Pour in heavy cream and stir with a fork until just combined.
4. Turn dough out onto a lightly floured surface and knead very gently just until it comes together.
5. Roll dough out to a 1-inch thickness and use a biscuit cutter to cut out circles.
6. Transfer to a parchment paper-lined baking sheet and bake for about 20 minutes, or until golden brown.
7. In a medium bowl, combine strawberries, sugar, melted butter, and lemon juice.
8. To assemble the shortcake, cut each biscuit in half and spoon a generous amount of the strawberry mixture on the bottom half of the biscuit. Top with the other half and enjoy!

Nutrition Information:
Calories: 350, Total Fat: 20 g, Sodium: 390 mg, Total Carbohydrate: 38 g, Fiber: 2 g, Sugars: 12 g, Protein: 4 g

59. lemon white chocolate cake

Indulge in this zesty yet sweet Lemon White Chocolate Cake! A delightful mix of tartness from the lemon and sweetness from the white chocolate will make this cake the highlight of any summer gathering.
Serving: 8
Preparation Time: 40 minutes
Ready Time: 1 hour

Ingredients:
- 1 3/4 cup cake flour
- 2 teaspoons baking powder
- 1/2 teaspoon of salt
- 1/2 cup of butter (at room temperature)
- 1 cup white sugar
- 2 eggs
- 2/3 cup milk
- 2 tablespoons lemon zest
- 1/2 teaspoon of lemon juice
- 3/4 cup white chocolate chips

Instructions:
1. Preheat oven to 350°F. Grease a 9-inch round cake pan and set aside.
2. In a medium bowl, whisk together the cake flour, baking powder and salt.
3. In a separate bowl, beat together the butter with the sugar with an electric mixer until light and fluffy. Beat in the eggs one at a time.
4. Alternate adding the dry Ingredients and the milk into the butter mixture. Beat until just combined.
5. Stir in the lemon zest and lemon juice. Fold in the white chocolate chips.
6. Pour the batter into the cake pan and bake in the preheated oven for 35-40 minutes, or until a cake tester comes out clean.
7. Let the cake cool in the pan for 15 minutes before removing and cooling it completely on a wire rack. Enjoy!

Nutrition Information:
Per Serving (1 slice): 508 calories; 23g fat; 65g carbohydrates; 5g protein.

60. lemon blueberry cream cheese cake

This Lemon Blueberry Cream Cheese Cake is a delicious balance of tart and sweet, with a creamy cream cheese custard layer that ties it all together. Serve this as a light, refreshing dessert that is sure to impress!
Serving: 8
Preparation Time: 15 minutes + 25-30 minutes baking time
Ready Time: 40-45 minutes

Ingredients:
-1/2 cup all-purpose flour
-1/2 teaspoon baking powder
-1/4 teaspoon baking soda
-1/4 teaspoon salt
-1/2 cup (1 stick) unsalted butter, at room temperature
-1/2 cup granulated sugar
-2 large eggs, at room temperature
-1 teaspoon pure vanilla extract
-1/4 teaspoon finely grated lemon zest
-1/4 cup fresh lemon juice
-1 cup fresh blueberries
-1/2 cup cream cheese, at room temperature

Instructions:
1. Preheat oven to 350°F. Grease and flour an 8-inch round cake pan.
2. In a medium bowl, whisk together the flour, baking powder, baking soda, and salt.
3. In a large bowl, beat the butter and sugar together until light and fluffy. Add the eggs one at a time, beating well after each addition. Add the vanilla extract, lemon zest, and lemon juice, and beat until combined.
4. Gradually add the dry Ingredients, and beat until just combined.
5. Gently fold in the blueberries.
6. In a separate bowl, beat the cream cheese until smooth.
7. Pour half of the cake batter into the prepared pan. Spread the cream cheese over the top evenly. Top with the remaining cake batter.
8. Bake for 25-30 minutes, or until a toothpick inserted into the center comes out clean.
9. Cool the cake completely before serving.

Nutrition Information: Calories: 307 kcal; Total Fat: 17 g; Saturated Fat: 10 g; Cholesterol: 87 mg; Sodium: 166 mg; Potassium: 80 mg; Carbohydrates: 33 g; Fiber: 1 g; Sugar: 23 g; Protein: 5 g

61. lemon chamomile cake

Lemon Chamomile Cake is a delightful dessert that combines the refreshing citrus flavor of lemons with the delicate floral notes of chamomile. This moist and fragrant cake is perfect for any occasion, whether it's a casual afternoon tea or a special celebration. The combination of zesty lemon and soothing chamomile creates a unique flavor profile that will surely impress your taste buds. Give this recipe a try and indulge in a slice of this heavenly cake!
Serving: 12 slices
Preparation time: 20 minutes
Ready time: 1 hour 30 minutes

Ingredients:
For the cake:
- 2 cups all-purpose flour
- 2 teaspoons baking powder
- 1/2 teaspoon baking soda
- 1/4 teaspoon salt
- 1 tablespoon chamomile tea leaves (dried or fresh)
- 1 cup unsalted butter, softened
- 1 1/2 cups granulated sugar
- 4 large eggs
- 1 teaspoon vanilla extract
- 1 tablespoon lemon zest
- 1/4 cup fresh lemon juice
- 1/2 cup buttermilk

For the lemon chamomile glaze:
- 1 cup powdered sugar
- 2 tablespoons fresh lemon juice
- 1 tablespoon chamomile tea leaves (dried or fresh)

Instructions:

1. Preheat your oven to 350°F (175°C) and grease a 9-inch round cake pan.
2. In a small bowl, combine the flour, baking powder, baking soda, salt, and chamomile tea leaves. Set aside.
3. In a large mixing bowl, cream together the softened butter and granulated sugar until light and fluffy.
4. Add the eggs, one at a time, beating well after each addition. Stir in the vanilla extract.
5. Add the lemon zest and lemon juice to the butter mixture and mix until well combined.
6. Gradually add the dry Ingredients to the wet Ingredients, alternating with the buttermilk. Begin and end with the dry Ingredients, mixing just until combined after each addition. Be careful not to overmix.
7. Pour the batter into the prepared cake pan and smooth the top with a spatula.
8. Bake in the preheated oven for 45-50 minutes, or until a toothpick inserted into the center of the cake comes out clean.
9. While the cake is baking, prepare the lemon chamomile glaze. In a small bowl, whisk together the powdered sugar, lemon juice, and chamomile tea leaves until smooth and well combined.
10. Once the cake is done, remove it from the oven and let it cool in the pan for 10 minutes. Then, transfer the cake to a wire rack to cool completely.
11. Drizzle the lemon chamomile glaze over the cooled cake, allowing it to drip down the sides.
12. Slice the Lemon Chamomile Cake and serve it as a delightful dessert or enjoy it with a cup of tea.

Nutrition Information (per serving):
- Calories: 320
- Total Fat: 14g
- Saturated Fat: 8g
- Cholesterol: 90mg
- Sodium: 210mg
- Total Carbohydrate: 47g
- Sugars: 30g
- Protein: 4g
- Vitamin C: 8%
- Calcium: 6%
- Iron: 8%

Note: The Nutrition Information is approximate and may vary depending on the specific Ingredients and quantities used.

62. lemon coconut cream cake

Lemon Coconut Cream Cake
Serving: 8-10
Preparation Time: 20 minutes
Ready Time: 1 hour

Ingredients:
- 1 package of lemon cake mix
- 3 eggs
- 1/3 cup of vegetable oil
- 1 1/3 cup of water
- 1 14 oz can of sweetened condensed milk
- 1/2 cup of lime juice
- 2 cups of shredded coconut
- 1 8 oz container of whipped cream

Instructions:
1. Preheat oven to 350°F. Grease a 9 x 13 inch baking pan.
2. In a large bowl, combine lemon cake mix, eggs, vegetable oil, and water. Mix until Ingredients are fully incorporated.
3. Pour cake batter into greased pan and bake for 25 minutes.
4. In a separate bowl, combine condensed milk and lime juice. Mix thoroughly.
5. When cake is done baking, spread condensed milk mixture over the top and sprinkle coconut over it.
6. Allow cake to cool for 30 minutes before adding the whipped cream.
7. Serve cooled cake. Enjoy!

Nutrition Information: Each serving contains 570 calories, 30g fat, 80g carbohydrates, and 8g protein.

63. lemon elderflower and raspberry cake

Lemon Elderflower and Raspberry Cake
Serving: 8 - 12
Preparation Time: 25 minutes
Ready Time: 1 hour and 45 minutes

Ingredients:
- 2/3 cup of butter (softened)
- 1 ½ cups of caster sugar
- 2 tablespoons of lemon zest
- 4 large eggs
- 7 ounces of self-raising flour
- 1 tablespoon of elderflower cordial
- 3 tablespoons of milk
- 2 cups of raspberries
- 2 tablespoons of flaked almonds

Instructions:
1. Preheat oven to 350 degrees F (175 degrees C)
2. Grease and flour an 8-inch cake pan
3. In a large bowl, cream together the butter, sugar and lemon zest until the mixture is light and fluffy
4. Beat in the eggs one at a time, mixing well after each one
5. Sift in the flour and gently fold in the mixture
6. Slowly stir in the elderflower cordial and the milk until the batter is just combined
7. Pour the batter into the prepared pan
8. Gently fold in the raspberries and sprinkle with flaked almonds
9. Bake in the preheated oven for 1 hour and 25 minutes, or until the cake is golden brown and a skewer inserted in the center comes out clean

Nutrition Information: Calories:349; Total Fat: 15g; Cholesterol: 67mg; Sodium: 229mg; Total Carbohydrates: 47g; Dietary Fiber: 2g; Protein: 4g

64. lemon and lavender honey cake

This delicious lemon and lavender honey cake is sure to be a hit with guests or the perfect dessert for any special occasion.

Serving: 16
Preparation Time: 15 minutes
Ready Time: 1 hour

Ingredients:
- 1/2 cup butter, softened
- 3/4 cup honey
- 1 teaspoon dried lavender
- 1 teaspoon lemon zest
- 2 eggs
- 1/2 teaspoon vanilla extract
- 1 cup all-purpose flour
- 1 teaspoon baking powder
- 1 pinch of salt

Instructions:
1. Preheat oven to 350°F (175°C). Grease and flour a 9-inch round baking pan.
2. In a medium bowl, cream together butter and honey until light and fluffy. Stir in lavender and lemon zest. Beat in eggs, one at a time, then stir in vanilla.
3. In a separate bowl, sift together flour, baking powder and salt. Gradually stir the dry Ingredients into the honey mixture, until just combined.
4. Pour the batter into the prepared pan. Bake in the preheated oven for 30 to 40 minutes, or until a toothpick inserted into the center of the cake comes out clean. Allow to cook in the pan for 10 minutes, then turn out onto a wire rack to cool.

Nutrition Information:
Serving size: 1 slice
Calories: 200
Total Fat: 8g
Total Carbohydrates: 30g
Protein: 2g

65. lemon matcha pound cake

Lemon Matcha Pound Cake
Serving: 10
Preparation Time: 20 minutes
Ready Time: 1 hour

Ingredients:
- 2 cups all-purpose flour
- 1 teaspoon baking powder
- 1/4 teaspoon baking soda
- 1/2 teaspoon salt
- 1 cup butter, room temperature
- 1 1/2 cups white sugar
- 4 eggs
- 1 teaspoon vanilla extract
- 1/4 cup freshly squeezed lemon juice
- 2 tablespoons matcha powder
- 1/2 cup sour cream

Instructions:
1. Preheat your oven to 350°F (175°C). Grease an 8 or 9 inch pound cake pan.
2. In a mixing bowl, sift together the flour, baking powder, baking soda, and salt.
3. In a separate bowl, cream together the butter and sugar until creamy.
4. Add the eggs one at a time, beating well after each addition.
5. To the wet Ingredients, add the vanilla extract, lemon juice, matcha powder, and sour cream.
6. Gradually add in the dry Ingredients, mixing until combined.
7. Pour the batter into the prepared cake pan.
8. Bake for 45-50 minutes, or until a toothpick inserted into the center comes out clean.
9. Let the cake cool for at least 15 minutes before transferring to a plate.

Nutrition Information:
Calories per serving: 500 calories
Fat per serving: 24 grams

66. lemon olive oil and thyme cake

This flavorful and moist lemon olive oil and thyme cake is a delicious and easy to make dessert that is sure to please any crowd.
Serving: 10
Preparation Time: 20 minutes
Ready Time: 1 hour and 15 minutes

Ingredients:
- 4 eggs
- 1 1/2 cups sugar
- 1 3/4 cups all-purpose flour
- 2 tablespoons lemon zest
- 1/4 teaspoon salt
- 1/2 teaspoon baking powder
- 1/2 teaspoon baking soda
- 1 cup olive oil
- 1/3 cup freshly squeezed lemon juice
- 2 teaspoons chopped fresh thyme
- 2 tablespoons powdered sugar for dusting

Instructions:
1. Preheat oven to 350 degrees F.
2. Grease and flour a 9x 13 inch baking pan.
3. In a large bowl, beat together the eggs and sugar until light and creamy.
4. In another bowl, mix together the flour, lemon zest, salt, baking powder, and baking soda.
5. Slowly pour the olive oil and lemon juice into the egg mixture and mix until combined.
6. Gradually add the dry Ingredients to the wet mixture and mix until just incorporated.
7. Pour the batter into the prepared baking pan.
8. Sprinkle with chopped thyme.
9. Bake for 40-50 minutes, or until a toothpick inserted in the center comes out clean.
10. Let cool in pan for 10 minutes, then remove and let cool completely.
11. Dust with powdered sugar and serve.

Nutrition Information:

Serving size: 1 slice
Calories: 279
Fat: 15g
Carbohydrates: 31g
Protein: 4g
Fiber: 1g

67. lemon peanut butter cake

This Lemon Peanut Butter Cake is a delightful twist on a classic cake. Sweet and tart, this all-in-one dessert has a peanut butter cake base, lemon curd filling, and an airy, nutty meringue frosting.
Serving: 8-10
Preparation Time: 30 minutes
Ready Time: 50 minutes

Ingredients:
- 2 1/4 cups all-purpose flour
- 1 1/2 teaspoon baking powder
- 1/2 teaspoon baking soda
- 1 teaspoon salt
- 1 cup creamy peanut butter
- 1 cup sugar
- 3/4 cup vegetable oil
- 3/4 cup milk
- 1 teaspoon vanilla extract
- 2 eggs
- 2 tablespoons freshly squeezed lemon juice
- 1/3 cup prepared lemon curd
- 5 large egg whites
- 3/4 cup white sugar
- 2 cups roughly chopped peanuts

Instructions:
1. Preheat oven to 350°F (175°C). Grease and flour a 9-inch round cake pan.
2. In a large bowl, whisk together flour, baking powder, baking soda, and salt.

3. In a separate bowl, cream together peanut butter, sugar, oil, and milk until light and fluffy.
4. Stir in vanilla extract, eggs, and lemon juice.
5. Slowly add the dry Ingredients to the wet Ingredients, and mix until just combined.
6. Pour batter into prepared pan and bake for 25-30 minutes or until a toothpick inserted into the center comes out clean.
7. Let cool for 10 minutes, and then remove from the pan and let cool completely.
8. Spread lemon curd on top of cake.
9. To prepare the meringue, in a large bowl, beat egg whites until soft peaks form. Slowly add sugar and beat until stiff peaks form.
10. Spread meringue over the cake. Sprinkle chopped peanuts over the meringue.
11. Place the cake under the broiler for a few minutes, until lightly golden.

Nutrition Information:
Serving size: 1 slice
Calories: 465 kcal
Fat: 22.3 g
Carbohydrates: 55.5 g
Protein: 11.1 g
Sodium: 483 mg

68. lemon poppyseed bundt cake

Lemon Poppyseed Bundt Cake – a moist, zesty, and nutty flavored pound cake that's a nice twist from the classic.
Serving: 8 - 10
Preparation Time: 30 minutes
Ready Time: 1 hour

Ingredients:
- 3 cups all-purpose flour
- 1 teaspoon baking powder
- 1/2 teaspoon baking soda
- 1/2 teaspoon salt

- 1/2 cup poppy seeds
- 1 cup unsalted butter, softened
- 2 cups granulated sugar
- 4 eggs
- 2 tablespoons fresh lemon juice
- 2 teaspoons grated lemon zest
- 1/2 cup sour cream
- 1 teaspoon vanilla extract

Instructions:
1. Preheat the oven to 350°F. Grease and flour a 10-inch tube pan.
2. In a large bowl, sift together the flour, baking powder, baking soda, and salt, then stir in the poppy seeds.
3. In the bowl of an electric mixer, cream together the butter and sugar until light and fluffy. Add the eggs one at a time, beating well after each addition.
4. Beat in the lemon juice, lemon zest, sour cream, and vanilla extract until just combined.
5. Gradually add the dry Ingredients to the wet, and mix until just combined.
6. Pour the batter into the prepared pan and bake for 45-50 minutes, or until a toothpick inserted in the center comes out clean. Let the cake cool in the pan for 10 minutes before turning it out onto a wire rack to cool completely.

Nutrition Information:
Each serving provides approximately 336 Calories, 5.6g protein, 19.2g fat, 36.9 carbohydrates, 6.2g dietary fibre, and 76.8mg cholesterol.

69. lemon raspberry cream cake

This Lemon Raspberry Cream Cake is the perfect sweet option for special occasions. A light sponge cake base is loaded with a sweet and tart raspberry cream cheese and topped with a tangy lemon curd.
Serving: 12
Preparation Time: 35 minutes
Ready Time: 2 hours and 20 minutes

Ingredients:
- 2 and 3/4 cups all-purpose flour
- 2 teaspoons baking powder
- 1/2 teaspoon baking soda
- 1 teaspoon salt
- 1 cup butter, softened
- 1 and 3/4 cups white sugar
- 4 large eggs
- 1 and 1/4 cups buttermilk
- 1 teaspoon vanilla extract
- 2 (8 ounce) packages cream cheese, softened
- 2 cups confectioners' sugar
- 2 tablespoons lemon juice
- 2 cups fresh raspberries
- 2 cups lemon curd

Instructions:
1. Preheat oven to 350 degrees F (175 degrees C). Grease and flour an 11-inch fluted Bundt pan.
2. In a large bowl, combine the flour, baking powder, baking soda and salt. In a separate bowl, cream together the butter and sugar until light and fluffy. Beat in the eggs one at a time, then stir in the vanilla. Beat in the flour mixture alternately with the buttermilk. Pour the batter into the prepared pan.
3. Bake for 45 minutes, or until a toothpick inserted comes out clean. Let cool in the pan for 10 minutes, then turn out onto a wire rack and cool completely.
4. For the filling, in a large bowl, mix together cream cheese and confectioners' sugar until smooth. Stir in the lemon juice. Gently fold in the raspberries. Mix in the lemon curd and spread the mixture over the top and sides of the cake.
5. Allow the cake to chill for 1 to 2 hours.

Nutrition Information:
Calories: 458 cal, Carbohydrates: 59 g, Protein: 6 g, Fat: 22.5 g, Saturated Fat: 13.7 g, Cholesterol: 97.4 mg, Sodium: 479.9 mg, Potassium: 177 mg, Fiber: 2.1 g, Sugar: 40.2 g, Vitamin A: 809.8 IU, Vitamin C: 22.5 mg, Calcium: 93.7 mg, Iron: 1.7 mg

70. lemon gingerbread bundt cake

Try this delicious Lemon Gingerbread Bundt Cake - a light and fluffy lemon cake infused with flavors of ginger and spices. This is the perfect dessert to pair with a hot cup of tea or your favorite cup of coffee.
Serving: 8-10
Preparation Time: 35 minutes
Ready Time: 1 hour and 15 minutes

Ingredients:
- 1/2 cup butter, softened
- 1 cup granulated sugar
- 2 eggs
- 1/4 cup sour cream
- 1 teaspoon grated fresh ginger
- 1 teaspoon vanilla
- 2 2/3 cups all-purpose flour
- 1 teaspoon baking powder
- 1/4 teaspoon baking soda
- 1/2 teaspoon salt
- 1/4 teaspoon ground nutmeg
- 1/2 teaspoon ground cinnamon
- 1/4 teaspoon ground allspice
- Grated zest of 1 lemon
- 1/2 cup warmed honey or molasses
- 1/2 cup buttermilk

Instructions:
1. Preheat the oven to 350 degrees Fahrenheit. Grease and flour a 9-inch bundt pan.
2. With an electric mixer, cream the butter and sugar until light and fluffy.
3. Add the eggs one at a time and mix until fully incorporated.
4. Add the sour cream, ginger, and vanilla and mix until combined.
5. In a separate bowl, whisk together the flour, baking powder, baking soda, salt, nutmeg, cinnamon, allspice, and lemon zest.
6. With the mixer on low, add half of the dry Ingredients to the wet Ingredients and mix until just combined.
7. Add the honey or molasses and mix until just combined.

8. Add the remaining dry Ingredients and buttermilk and mix until just combined.
9. Pour the batter into the prepared bundt pan.
10. Bake for 35 minutes or until a tester inserted into the center of the cake comes out clean.
11. Let cool in the pan for 10 minutes before carefully turning out onto a cooling rack to cool completely.

Nutrition Information:
Calories - 259 kcal, Fat - 9 g, Carbohydrates - 39 g, Protein - 3 g, Cholesterol - 58 mg, Sodium - 129 mg, Potassium - 72 mg, Fiber - 1 g, Sugar - 20 g

71. lemon and rosemary olive oil cake

Lemon and Rosemary Olive Oil Cake - This simple, delicious, and fragrant cake is sure to impress your guests. Infused with the herbal flavor of rosemary and lime zest, and moist with light olive oil, this cake is a delightful addition to any table.
Serving - 8-10
Preparation Time - 20 minutes
Ready Time - 1 hour

Ingredients:
- 2 cups all-purpose flour
- 1 teaspoon baking powder
- 1/4 teaspoon salt
- 1 3/4 cups sugar
- zest of 3 large lemons
- 3 tablespoons fresh rosemary, finely chopped
- 1 cup light olive oil
- 4 eggs
- 1/2 cup water

Instructions:
1. Preheat the oven to 350°F (175°C). Grease and flour a 9-inch (23 cm) cake pan.
2. In a large bowl, combine the flour, baking powder, salt, and sugar.

3. Add the lemon zest, rosemary, and olive oil and mix until combined.
4. Beat in the eggs one at a time until fully incorporated.
5. Gradually mix in the water to make a batter.
6. Pour the batter into the prepared pan and bake for 40–50 minutes, or until a toothpick inserted into the center comes out clean.
7. Allow to cool for 10 minutes before serving.

Nutrition Information
Calories - 225
Fat - 11.8 g
Carbohydrates - 28.1 g
Protein - 3.4 g
Sugar - 12.9 g

72. lemon and strawberry parfait cake

Get away with a delicious twist to the classic cake with this Lemon and Strawberry Parfait Cake. A great treat to serve to friends and family, the combination of lemon and strawberries creates a flavor explosion that will leave them wanting more!
Serving: Serves 7-8
Preparation Time: 30 minutes
Ready Time: 3 hours, 30 minutes

Ingredients:
- 2 cups all-purpose flour
- 1 teaspoon baking powder
- ½ teaspoon baking soda
- ½ teaspoon salt
- ¼ cup fresh lemon juice
- 1 teaspoon lemon zest
- 2 eggs
- ½ cup granulated sugar
- ½ cup butter, melted
- 2 tablespoons vegetable oil
- ½ teaspoon vanilla extract
- ⅓ cup buttermilk
- 2 cups strawberries, sliced

- 2 tablespoons powdered sugar

Instructions:
1. Preheat oven to 350°F (180°C). Grease a 9-inch springform pan with butter and lightly dust with all-purpose flour.
2. In a medium bowl, whisk together the flour, baking powder, baking soda, and salt.
3. In a separate bowl, whisk together the lemon juice, lemon zest, eggs, sugar, melted butter, vegetable oil, and vanilla extract until combined. Gradually add in the dry Ingredients and mix until a thick batter is formed. Add the buttermilk and mix until incorporated.
4. Pour the batter into the prepared pan and bake for 25-30 minutes, or until a toothpick inserted in the center of the cake comes out clean. Allow the cake to cool completely.
5. Once the cake has cooled, spread the sliced strawberries on top and sprinkle with the powdered sugar. Carefully remove the cake from the pan, slice into wedges, and serve.

Nutrition Information:
Serving size: 1 slice (54 g)
Calories: 256 kcal
Fat: 12 g
Carbohydrates: 35
Protein: 3 g
Sugar: 18 g

73. lemon blackberry and honey cake

Lemon Blackberry and Honey Cake
Serving: 8
Preparation Time: 15 minutes
Ready Time: 1 hour 15 minutes

Ingredients:
- 3/4 cup unsalted butter, at room temperature
- 1 1/2 cups white sugar
- 2 eggs
- 2 teaspoons of grated lemon zest

- 1 tablespoon fresh lemon juice
- 1 teaspoon vanilla extract
- 2 cups all-purpose flour
- 2 teaspoons baking powder
- 1 teaspoon baking soda
- 3/4 cup buttermilk
- 2 cups blackberries
- 1/4 cup honey

Instructions:
1. Preheat oven to 350° Fahrenheit. Grease and flour 9-inch springform pan.
2. In a medium bowl, cream together butter and sugar using an electric mixer until light and fluffy. Add in eggs one at a time, beating each until fully incorporated. Mix in lemon zest, lemon juice, and vanilla.
3. In a separate bowl, mix together flour, baking powder, and baking soda. Gradually add in dry Ingredients to the wet mixture, alternating with the buttermilk, beginning and ending with the dry Ingredients.
4. Spread half of the batter into the prepared baking pan. Top with blackberries, gently pressing them into the batter. Drizzle with honey, then top with remaining batter.
5. Bake for 1 hour, or until a toothpick inserted into the center of cake comes out clean. Let cool completely before removing from pan.

Nutrition Information:
Serving size: 1 slice
Calories: 375 kcal
Fat: 14 g
Carbohydrates: 57 g
Protein: 4 g

74. lemon coconut and mango cake

This Lemon Coconut and Mango Cake is a tasty tropical-inspired dessert that is sure to bring a smile to the face of anyone who takes a piece. This zesty cake has a refreshing lemon flavor, sweet coconut, and luscious mango pieces added in for an extra burst of flavor.
Serving: 10-12

Preparation Time: 20 minutes
Ready Time: 1 hour 10 minutes

Ingredients:
- 2 1/2 cups all-purpose flour
- 2 teaspoons baking powder
- 1/2 teaspoon baking soda
- 1/2 teaspoon salt
- 1/2 cup butter, softened
- 1 cup granulated sugar
- 3 large eggs
- 1 teaspoon vanilla extract
- 1 cup plain yogurt
- Zest of 2 lemons
- 1/4 cup freshly squeezed lemon juice
- 1 cup sweetened flaked coconut
- 1/2 cup diced mango

Instructions:
1. Preheat oven to 350 degrees Fahrenheit. Grease and flour a 9x13 inch baking pan.
2. In a medium bowl, whisk together flour, baking powder, baking soda, and salt. Set aside.
3. In a large bowl, beat butter and sugar until creamy. Add eggs one at a time, mixing after each addition. Add vanilla, yogurt, and lemon zest and mix until combined.
4. Add dry Ingredients to wet Ingredients and mix until just combined. Add lemon juice and mix until incorporated.
5. Fold in coconut and mango until combined.
6. Pour batter into prepared baking pan. Bake for 40-45 minutes, or until a toothpick inserted into the center comes out clean.
7. Let cool for 10 minutes before serving.

Nutrition Information:
Serving Size: 1 slice,
Calories: 240 kcal,
Total Fat: 10 g,
Saturated fat: 7 g,
Trans Fat: 0 g,
Cholesterol: 41 mg,

Sodium: 181 mg,
Total Carbohydrate: 33 g,
Dietary Fiber: 1 g,
Sugars: 20 g,
Protein: 4 g.

75. lemon and orange upside-down cake

This citrusy dessert is the perfect way to end any meal. A sweet cake with tart lemon and orange slices and topped off with a sticky glaze, this lemon and orange upside-down cake is bound to make a statement.
Serving: 10
Preparation Time: 35 minutes
Ready Time: 1 hour 20 minutes

Ingredients:
- ¾ cup melted butter
- 1 ½ cups packed light or dark brown sugar
- 2 lemon slices, each cut into 8 wedges
- 6 orange slices, each cut into 4 wedges
- 3 eggs
- 2 cups all-purpose flour
- 2 teaspoons baking powder
- ½ teaspoon salt
- 2 teaspoons vanilla extract
- ½ cup milk
- 1 teaspoon grated lemon zest
- 1 teaspoon grated orange zest
- 2 tablespoons melted butter

Instructions:
1. Preheat oven to 350°F (175°C). Grease a 9-inch (23 cm) springform cake pan.
2. In a medium bowl, combine melted butter and brown sugar. Spread this mixture in the cake pan. Arrange lemon and orange slices on top of the mixture.
3. In a separate bowl, beat eggs until creamy. Add flour, baking powder, salt, and vanilla extract to the egg mixture and mix until incorporated.

4. Slowly stir in milk, lemon zest, orange zest, and melted butter until everything is fully combined.
5. Pour cake batter over the citrus slices and spread evenly. Bake in preheated oven for 45 minutes. Allow to cool before removing from pan.

Nutrition Information: Calorie: 295, Carbohydrates: 46g, Protein: 4g, Fat: 10g, Saturated Fat: 6g, Cholesterol: 58mg, Sodium: 251mg, Potassium: 150mg, Fiber: 1g, Sugar: 31g, Vitamin A: 319IU, Vitamin C: 8.7mg, Calcium: 70mg, Iron: 1.9mg.

76. lemon buttermilk cake

Lemon Buttermilk Cake
Serving: 8
Preparation Time: 20 min
Ready Time: 50 min

Ingredients:
- 2 1/2 cups all-purpose flour
- 2 teaspoons baking powder
- 1/2 teaspoon baking soda
- 1 teaspoon salt
- 1/2 cup butter, at room temperature
- 1 1/2 cups granulated sugar
- 3 large eggs
- 1/3 cup strained fresh lemon juice
- 2 teaspoons pure vanilla extract
- 1 teaspoon finely grated lemon zest
- 3/4 cup buttermilk

Instructions:
1. Preheat oven to 350°F. Grease a 9-inch round cake pan.
2. In a medium bowl, whisk together the flour, baking powder, baking soda, and salt.
3. In a medium bowl with an electric mixer, beat the butter for 1 minute until light and fluffy. Gradually add the sugar and beat for 2 minutes until combined.

4. Scrape down the side of the bowl. Add the eggs one at a time and beat for 1 minute between each addition.
5. Beat in the lemon juice, vanilla, and lemon zest until just combined.
6. With the mixer on low speed, add in the dry Ingredients in three parts, alternating with the buttermilk in two parts. Beat until just combined and no streaks of flour remain.
7. Scrape the batter into the prepared pan and spread in an even layer.
8. Bake for 40-50 minutes, or until golden and a toothpick inserted into the center of the cake comes out with a few moist crumbs.
9. Cool completely before removing from pan.

Nutrition Information:
Calories: 507, Fat: 18 g, Saturated Fat: 11 g, Cholesterol: 82 mg, Sodium: 532 mg, Potassium: 178 mg, Carbohydrates: 79 g, Fiber: 1 g, Sugar: 47 g, Protein: 8 g, Vitamin A: 557 IU, Vitamin C: 7 mg, Calcium: 126 mg, Iron: 2 mg

77. lemon and pistachio pound cake

Lemon and Pistachio Pound Cake
Serving: 10 slices
Preparation Time: 15 minutes
Ready Time: 1 hour

Ingredients:
- 2 ½ cups all-purpose flour
- 1 teaspoon baking powder
- ½ teaspoon baking soda
- ½ teaspoon salt
- 1 cup butter, room temperature
- 2 cups granulated sugar
- 4 large eggs
- 2 teaspoons vanilla extract
- 1 cup buttermilk
- ¼ cup fresh lemon juice
- Grated zest of 2 lemons
- ¾ cup unsalted shelled pistachios, coarsely chopped

Instructions:
1. Preheat the oven to 350°F and butter a 9-inch loaf pan.
2. In a medium bowl, sift together the flour, baking powder, baking soda, and salt; set aside.
3. In a large bowl, cream together the butter and sugar until light and fluffy. Beat in the eggs one at a time, then add the vanilla, lemon juice, and lemon zest.
4. Gradually mix in the flour mixture, alternating with the buttermilk, until completely combined. Gently stir in the pistachios.
5. Pour the batter into the prepared pan and bake for 60 minutes, or until a toothpick inserted into the center comes out clean.
6. Cool cake on a wire rack before serving.

Nutrition Information:
Calories: 288 kcal, Carbohydrates: 38 g, Protein: 5 g, Fat: 13 g, Saturated Fat: 7 g, Cholesterol: 71 mg, Sodium: 219 mg, Potassium: 108 mg, Fiber: 1 g, Sugar: 23 g, Vitamin A: 410 IU, Vitamin C: 2 mg, Calcium: 50 mg, Iron: 1 mg

78. lemon and ricotta cake

Lemon and Ricotta Cake
Serving: 8-10
Preparation Time: 25 minutes
Ready Time: 1 hour

Ingredients:
- 2 & 1/2 cups all-purpose flour
- 2 teaspoons baking powder
- 1 & 1/2 teaspoons baking soda
- Pinch of salt
- 3/4 cup granulated sugar
- 1 cup ricotta cheese
- Zest of 1 lemon
- 2 eggs, room temperature
- 6 tablespoons butter, melted and cooled
- 1 teaspoon vanilla extract
- 2 teaspoons lemon extract

- 2/3 cup buttermilk

Instructions:
1. Preheat oven to 350°F (175°C). Grease an 8 or 9-inch baking pan and set aside.
2. Add the flour, baking powder, baking soda, and salt to a bowl and whisk together until combined.
3. In a separate bowl, add the sugar, ricotta cheese, lemon zest, eggs, melted butter, vanilla extract, and lemon extract. Mix until creamy.
4. Add the wet Ingredients to the dry Ingredients and mix until combined. Slowly add the buttermilk, mixing until the batter is smooth.
5. Pour the batter into the prepared baking pan. Bake for 45-50 minutes or until a toothpick inserted in the center comes out clean.
6. Allow the cake to cool completely before serving.

Nutrition Information:
Calories: 350; Protein: 7g; Fat: 11g; Carbohydrates: 53g; Sodium: 333mg; Cholesterol: 35mg; Fiber: 1g; Sugars: 24g

79. lemon and strawberry marble cake

Lemon and Strawberry Marble Cake
Serving: 12
Preparation Time: 20 minutes
Ready Time: 1 hour

Ingredients:
-1 ½ cups all-purpose flour
-2 teaspoons baking powder
-1 teaspoon baking soda
-pinch of salt
-½ cup (1 stick) butter, softened
-1 ¼ cup granulated sugar
-2 eggs
-1 teaspoon vanilla extract
-1 cup buttermilk
-½ teaspoon red food coloring
-½ teaspoon yellow food coloring

-1 lemon, zest only
-2 tablespoons freshly squeezed lemon juice
-1 cup diced strawberries

Instructions:
1. Preheat oven to 350 degrees F. Grease an 8-inch round cake pan and set aside.
2. In a medium bowl, whisk together the flour, baking powder, baking soda, and salt.
3. In a large bowl, cream together the butter and sugar until light and fluffy. Beat in eggs one at a time. Add in the vanilla extract.
3. Alternately add the buttermilk and flour mixture to the butter mixture, beginning and ending with the flour mixture.
4. Divide the batter evenly between two bowls. Add the red food coloring and yellow food coloring to each bowl, and mix until the batter is evenly colored.
5. Add the lemon zest and lemon juice to one of the bowls of batter.
6. Alternately spoon each color of batter into the cake pan. Place the diced strawberries on top.
7. Bake for 40-50 minutes, or until a toothpick inserted into the center of the cake comes out clean.
8. Allow to cool in the pan for 10 minutes before transferring to a serving plate.

Nutrition Information:
Total Calories: 262
Total Fat: 10.2g
Carbohydrates: 36.7g
Protein: 4.3g

80. lemon and white chocolate bundt cake

Lemon and White Chocolate Bundt Cake
Serving: 10-12
Preparation Time: 15 minutes
Ready Time: 55 minutes

Ingredients:

- 1/2 cup butter, softened
- 1 1/2 cups granulated sugar
- 3 eggs
- 1 teaspoon vanilla
- 1 1/3 cups all-purpose flour
- 1/2 teaspoon baking powder
- 1/4 teaspoon baking soda
- 1/4 teaspoon salt
- 1/2 cup sour cream
- 2 tablespoons grated lemon zest
- 2 tablespoons freshly squeezed lemon juice
- 3/4 cup white chocolate chips

Instructions:
1. Preheat oven to 350 degrees. Grease and flour a 10-12 cup bundt pan.
2. In a medium bowl, beat the butter and sugar until creamed together. Add the eggs one at a time until fully incorporated.
3. Add in the vanilla, flour, baking powder, baking soda, and salt. Mix until blended.
4. Slowly add in the sour cream, lemon zest and juice, and white chocolate chips. Mix until fully combined.
5. Pour the batter into the prepared bundt pan and bake for about 45-55 minutes, or until a tester inserted into the center of the cake comes out clean.
6. Allow to cool in the tin for 10 minutes before transferring to a cooling rack.

Nutrition Information:
Calories: 300kcal, Carbohydrates: 41g, Protein: 3.5g, Fat: 11.5g, Saturated Fat: 7g, cholesterol: 51mg, Sodium: 270mg, Potassium: 48mg, Fiber: 1g, Sugar: 24g, Vitamin A: 7.3%, Vitamin C: 1.2%, Calcium: 5%, Iron: 2.2%.

81. lemon and raspberry drizzle cake

This lemon and raspberry drizzle cake is a moist and delicious cake that is perfectly sweet with a hint of tartness. With its subtle flavors and light texture, this cake is sure to become a favorite.
Serving: 6-8

Preparation Time: 30 minutes
Ready Time: 1 hour 30 minutes

Ingredients:
- 3 large eggs
- 1/3 cup vegetable oil
- 1/2 cup sour cream
- 2 cups self-rising flour
- 1/2 cup sugar
- Zest and juice of 1 lemon
- 2/3 cup frozen raspberries
- 1/2 cup icing sugar

Instructions:
1. Preheat oven to 350°F (175°C). Grease and line with parchment paper a 9 inch (23 cm) round cake tin.
2. In a large bowl, beat together the eggs, oil, sour cream, self-rising flour, sugar and lemon zest until just mixed.
3. Add the juice from 1 lemon and the frozen raspberries into the mixture. Spoon into the prepared tin and level the surface.
4. Bake in preheated oven for about 50 minutes, or until a toothpick inserted in the center comes out clean.
5. When the cake is done, let cool on a wire rack.
6. Make the drizzle topping by sifting the icing sugar into a small bowl and adding 2-3 tablespoons of the reserved lemon juice until the mix is of a drizzling consistency.
7. Drizzle the lemon and icing sugar mixture over the cooled cake and serve.

Nutrition Information:
Calories – 276 kcal, Protein – 5g, Fat – 8.2g, Carbohydrate – 45.7g, Sugar – 22.3g

82. lemon and elderflower drizzle cake

This delicious lemon and elderflower drizzle cake is a perfect combination of sweet and tart flavors. It is light and airy and perfect for any occasion.

Serving: 8
Preparation Time: 40 minutes
Ready Time: 2 hours

Ingredients:
  3/4 cup butter, softened
- 1 1/2 cups granulated sugar
- 2 tablespoons lemon zest
- 2 teaspoons elderflower concentrate
- 4 eggs
- 2 cups self-raising flour
- 2/3 cup milk
- 2 tablespoons of elderflower liqueur
- 1/4 cup icing sugar
- Juice of 1 lemon

Instructions:
1. Preheat oven to 350 degrees F. Line an 8-inch cake tin with parchment paper.
2. Cream together butter and sugar until light and fluffy.
3. Add lemon zest and elderflower concentrate and mix.
4. Beat in eggs one at a time.
5. Gradually add flour and milk, alternating between the two.
6. Pour batter into cake tin and bake for 35-40 minutes or until a toothpick inserted in the center comes out clean.
7. In a small bowl, whisk together the elderflower liqueur, icing sugar and lemon juice.
8. Once the cake is slightly cooled, poke holes in the top using a fork and pour the lemon and elderflower syrup over it.

Nutrition Information: per serving; Calories: 440, Fat: 19g, Carbs: 59g, Protein: 5g

83. lemon and blueberry custard cake

This mouthwatering lemon and blueberry custard cake is a delightful infusion of tangy, sweet, and creamy flavors. Prepared with a lemony

sponge cake base, creamy custard center, and topped with fresh blueberries, it is sure to please the taste buds!
Serving: Serves 8
Preparation time: 25 minutes
Ready time: 1 hour

Ingredients:
- 4 eggs
- ¾ cup granulated sugar
- 1½ cups all-purpose flour
- 2 teaspoons baking powder
- ½ teaspoon salt
- 1 teaspoon lemon zest
- ⅓ cup vegetable oil
- ½ cup whole milk
- ⅓ cup fresh lemon juice
- 2 cups custard
- 1 cup fresh blueberries

Instructions:
1. Preheat the oven to 350°F. Grease a 9-inch cake pan.
2. In a large bowl, beat the eggs with the sugar until light and fluffy.
3. In a separate bowl, mix the flour, baking powder, and salt. Add it to the egg mixture, stirring to combine.
4. Stir in the lemon zest, oil, milk, and lemon juice.
5. Pour the batter into the prepared cake pan.
6. Bake for 25 minutes, or until a toothpick inserted in the middle comes out clean.
7. Let the cake cool completely before adding the custard and fresh blueberries.
8. Slice and serve.

Nutrition Information:
Calories: 318, Total Fat: 13g, Saturated Fat: 4g, Cholesterol: 80mg, Sodium: 267mg, Total Carbohydrate: 44g, Dietary Fibre: 2g, Sugars: 24g, Protein: 6g.

84. lemon and thyme drizzle cake

Lemon & Thyme Drizzle Cake
Serving: 8 slices
Preparation time: 25 minutes
Ready time: 55 minutes

Ingredients:
- 150g self-raising flour
- 150g caster sugar
- 2 lemons
- 14g tub thyme
- 3 large eggs
- 150g Greek yogurt
- 85g butter, melted
- 1 tsp baking powder

Instructions:
1. Preheat oven to 180C/160C Fan/Gas Mark 4.
2. Grease and line a 20cm round cake tin with baking parchment.
3. In a large bowl, mix the self-raising flour, caster sugar, baking powder, and grated rind of one of the lemons.
4. In a small bowl, mix the Greek yogurt, melted butter, eggs, thyme and juice of one of the lemons.
5. Pour the wet Ingredients into the dry Ingredients and stir to combine.
6. Pour the cake mix into the greased tin and spread evenly.
7. Bake in preheated oven for 30 minutes or until a skewer inserted comes out clean.
8. Remove from oven and leave to cool for 10 minutes.
9. Drizzle the juice of the remaining lemon and a sprinkling of thyme over the top of the cake.
10. Enjoy!

Nutrition Information per slice:
Calories: 237Kcal
Carbohydrates: 31.3g
Sugars: 18.6g
Protein: 4.7g
Fat: 9.4g
Saturated Fat: 5.4g

Fibre: 0.6g

85. lemon and poppyseed layer cake

Lemon and Poppyseed Layer Cake
Serving: 8
Preparation Time: 30 minutes
Ready Time: 1 hour

Ingredients:
1 ½ cups all-purpose flour
½ cup white sugar
1 teaspoon baking powder
¼ teaspoon salt
2 tablespoons poppy seeds
2 eggs
½ cup freshly-squeezed lemon juice
½ cup vegetable oil
½ teaspoon vanilla extract
Frosting:
3 tablespoons freshly-squeezed lemon juice
3 ½ cups confectioners' sugar

Instructions:
1. Preheat oven to 350°F. Grease and line two round 9-inch cake pans.
2. In a bowl, stir together the flour, sugar, baking powder, salt, and poppy seeds.
3. In another bowl, beat eggs briefly, then stir in lemon juice, vegetable oil, and vanilla. Slowly incorporate the dry Ingredients into the wet mixture. Stir until combined.
4. Pour batter evenly into the prepared pans. Bake for 20 minutes or until a toothpick inserted in the center comes out clean. Cool in the pans for 15 minutes.
5. To make the frosting, whisk together the lemon juice and confectioners' sugar until smooth. Spread frosting between layers and over the top and sides of the cake.
6. Serve and enjoy!

Nutrition Information:
Calories: 340kcal, Carbohydrates: 57.3g, Protein: 3.5g, Fat: 10.7g, Saturated Fat: 9.4g, Cholesterol: 41mg, Sodium: 80mg, Potassium: 68mg, Sugar: 44.3g, Vitamin A: 67IU, Vitamin C: 2mg, Calcium: 30mg, Iron: .43mg

86. vegan lemon cake

Vegan Lemon Cake
Serving: 8-10
Preparation Time: 25 minutes
Ready Time: 1 hour

Ingredients:
- 1¼ cup all-purpose flour
- 1 cup granulated sugar
- 1 teaspoon baking powder
- 1 teaspoon baking soda
- 1/2 teaspoon salt
- 1/3 cup sunflower oil
- 3/4 cup vegan butter, melted
- 2 teaspoons vanilla extract
- 2/3 cup aquafaba (the liquid from a can of chickpeas)
- 2 tablespoons freshly squeezed lemon juice
- 2 tablespoons lemon zest
- 1/3 cup vegan milk

Instructions:
1. Preheat the oven to 350°F (175°C). Lightly grease and flour a 9 inch round cake pan.
2. In a medium bowl, whisk together the flour, sugar, baking powder, baking soda, and salt until evenly combined.
3. In a separate bowl, mix together the sunflower oil, melted vegan butter, vanilla extract, aquafaba, lemon juice, and lemon zest until combined.
4. Slowly add the wet Ingredients to the dry Ingredients and mix until just combined.
5. Add the vegan milk and mix until the batter is smooth.

6. Pour the batter into the prepared pan and bake for 30-35 minutes, or until a toothpick inserted into the center comes out clean. Let cool for 10 minutes before removing from pan.
7. Let cool completely before serving. Enjoy!

Nutrition Information:
Serving Size: 1 slice
Calories: 300
Carbohydrates: 35g
Protein: 4g
Fat: 16g
Saturated Fat: 2g
Cholesterol: 0mg
Sodium: 200mg
Potassium: 120mg
Fiber: 2g
Sugar: 28g
Vitamin A: 0.4%
Vitamin C: 2.3%
Calcium: 2.4%
Iron: 5.2%

87. gluten-free lemon cake

Description
Gluten-Free Lemon Cake is the perfect way to indulge a sweet tooth without having to worry about consuming gluten. With its light and airy lemon-infused sponge and decadent lemon glaze, this gluten-free cake will be the star of the dessert table.
Serving: 10
Preparation Time: 10 minutes
Ready Time: 25 minutes

Ingredients:
1 1/2 cups gluten-free flour
3 teaspoons baking powder
1/2 teaspoon baking soda
1/4 teaspoon salt

1/2 cup butter, softened
2/3 cup white sugar
2 eggs
2 teaspoons lemon zest
2 tablespoons fresh lemon juice
1/2 cup milk
Lemon Glaze:
3/4 cup icing sugar
2 tablespoons fresh lemon juice

Instructions:
1. Preheat oven to 350F. Grease an 8 inch round cake pan and line it with parchment paper.
2. In a medium bowl, whisk together the gluten-free flour, baking powder, baking soda, and salt.
3. In a large bowl, beat together the butter and sugar until light and fluffy. Beat in the eggs, one at a time, until well combined. Stir in the lemon zest and juice.
4. Alternate adding the milk and the dry Ingredients to the wet Ingredients, stirring just until combined.
5. Pour the batter into the prepared pan and spread evenly. Bake in preheated oven for 20-25 minutes or until a toothpick inserted in the center comes out clean.
6. Make the glaze: in a small bowl, whisk together icing sugar and lemon juice until smooth.
7. When the cake has cooled, drizzle the glaze over the top of the cake.

Nutrition Information:
Serving Size: 1 slice
Calories: 253 kcal
Total Fat: 10 g
Saturated Fat: 6 g
Cholesterol: 62 mg
Sodium: 217 mg
Total Carbohydrates: 36 g
Dietary Fiber: 1 g
Sugars: 23 g
Protein: 4 g

88. paleo lemon cake

Enjoy this light and moist Paleo Lemon Cake - this delicious paleo-friendly dessert will brighten up any gathering!
Serving: 8-10
Preparation Time: 10 minutes
Ready Time: 65 minutes

Ingredients:
- 2 cups almond flour
- 1 tsp baking soda
- ½ tsp salt
- 3 eggs
- 1 cup coconut sugar
- ½ cup melted coconut oil
- ½ cup almond milk
- Juice from 1 lemon
- 1 cup fresh blueberries

Instructions:
1. Preheat oven to 350°F (175°C). Grease an 8 inch (20 cm) cake pan with coconut oil.
2. In a large bowl, combine almond flour, baking soda, and salt.
3. In a separate bowl, whisk the eggs, then whisk in the coconut sugar and melted coconut oil.
4. Add the almond milk and lemon juice to the wet mixture, and whisk until combined.
5. Pour the wet Ingredients into the dry Ingredients, and mix until combined.
6. Gently fold in the blueberries, and pour the cake batter into the prepared pan.
7. Bake for 55 minutes, or until a toothpick inserted in the center comes out clean.
8. Remove from oven and let cool in pan for 10 minutes, then turn out onto a cooling rack and cool completely before serving.

Nutrition Information: Serving size: 1 slice (1/8 of the cake); Calories: 224; Fat: 15.5 g; Carbohydrates: 18.5 g; Protein: 5.2 g; Fiber: 2.2 g; Sugar: 12.3 g

89. keto lemon cake

Keto Lemon Cake
Serving: 8
Preparation time: 15 minutes
Ready time: 45 minutes

Ingredients:
- 1¼ cups almond flour
- 1 teaspoon baking powder
- ½ teaspoon sea salt
- 3 large eggs
- 3 tablespoons fresh lemon juice
- ½ cup Swerve (or monk fruit) sweetener
- 3 tablespoons butter, melted
- 1 teaspoon lemon zest

Instructions:
1. Preheat your oven to 350 degrees Fahrenheit and grease an 8-inch-by-8-inch cake pan with butter or cooking spray.
2. In a large bowl, combine the almond flour, baking powder, and sea salt. Mix together until the batter is well incorporated.
3. In a small bowl, whisk together the eggs, lemon juice, Swerve sweetener, melted butter, and lemon zest.
4. Pour the wet Ingredients into the dry Ingredients and mix until the batter is smooth.
5. Pour the batter into the prepared cake pan and bake for 30-35 minutes, or until a toothpick inserted into the center comes out clean.
6. Allow the cake to cool in the pan for 10 minutes before transferring to a cooling rack to cool completely.

Nutrition Information:
Serving size: 1 slice of cake (1/8 of entire cake)
Calories: 183
Total Fat: 15.6 g
Saturated Fat: 5.3 g
Cholesterol: 93.5 mg
Sodium: 223 mg

Carbohydrates: 7.7 g
Fiber: 2.5 g
Sugar: 1.2 g
Protein: 5.5 g

90. low-fat lemon cake

Indulge in a yummy, low-fat lemon cake that is perfect for any occasion.
Serving: 8
Preparation time: 15 minutes
Ready time: 45 minutes

Ingredients:
-1 ½ cup all-purpose flour
-½ cup brown sugar
-1 teaspoon baking powder
-1/4 teaspoon baking soda
-1/4 teaspoon salt
-1/3 cup freshly squeezed lemon juice
-2 tablespoons lemon zest
-2 tablespoons vegetable oil
-2 tablespoons chopped almonds
-1/2 cup low-fat yoghurt

Instructions:
1. Preheat oven to 350°F. Grease and flour an 8-inch round cake pan
2. Sift together the flour, baking powder, baking soda, and salt.
3. Stir in the sugar and almonds.
4. Beat in the lemon juice, lemon zest, vegetable oil, and yoghurt.
5. Pour the batter into the prepared pan and bake for 40 minutes or until a toothpick inserted in the middle comes out clean.
6. Let it cool before serving.

Nutrition Information:
Calories: 164
Total fat: 5g
Saturated fat: 2g
Trans fat: 0g

Cholesterol: 2mg
Sodium: 83mg
Total carbohydrates: 28g
Dietary fiber: 0.5g
Sugars: 14.5g
Protein: 3.75g

91. lemon and lime drizzle bundt cake

Lemon and Lime Drizzle Bundt Cake
Serving: 8-10
Preparation Time: 30 minutes
Ready Time: 1 hour (including cooling time)

Ingredients:
- 2 cups all-purpose flour
- 2 tsp baking powder
- 1/2 tsp baking soda
- 1/2 tsp salt
- 2/3 cup unsalted butter, melted
- 1 cup granulated sugar
- 2 large eggs
- 1/2 cup sour cream
- Zest of 2 lime
- Zest of 1 lemon
- Juice of 2 lime
- Juice of 1 lemon
- 1/2 cup powdered sugar

Instructions:
1. Preheat oven to 350 F. Grease and flour a 9-inch Bundt cake pan.
2. In a medium bowl, whisk together the flour, baking powder, baking soda, and salt.
3. In a large bowl, whisk together the melted butter and sugar until creamy. Add in the eggs one at a time, whisking in between each addition.
4. Whisk in the sour cream, and then stir in the zests of the lime and lemon.

5. Gradually add the dry Ingredients to the wet Ingredients, stirring until just combined.
6. Pour the batter into the prepared Bundt cake pan and bake for 35 to 40 minutes, or until a toothpick comes out clean.
7. Let cool in the pan for 10 minutes before turning out onto a cooling rack.
8. Meanwhile, make the drizzle by mixing both juices together in a small bowl with the powdered sugar. Drizzle the drizzle over the cooled cake.

Nutrition Information (Per Serving): 115 calories; 5 g fat; 1 g saturated fat; 17 g carbohydrates; 1 g protein; 46 mg sodium; 18 mg cholesterol.

92. lemon and rosemary cake with mascarpone frosting

This delightful lemon and rosemary cake with mascarpone frosting makes for the perfect sweet treat with punchy flavor.
Serving: Serves 8-10
Preparation Time: 20 minutes
Ready Time: 2 hours

Ingredients:
-Cake:
-3 cups all purpose flour
-1 teaspoon baking powder
-½ teaspoon baking soda
-¼ teaspoon salt
-2 tablespoons finely chopped fresh rosemary
-1 cup (2 sticks) unsalted butter, at room temperature
-2 cups granulated sugar
-4 large eggs
-1 teaspoon vanilla
-1 cup sour cream
-Grated zest of 1 lemon
Frosting:
-1 cup mascarpone cheese
-1 cup heavy cream

-3 tablespoons powdered sugar

Instructions:
Cake:
1. Preheat oven to 350°F. Grease and flour two 9-inch round cake pans.
2. In a medium bowl, whisk together flour, baking powder, baking soda, salt, and chopped rosemary; set aside.
3. In a large bowl, cream together butter and sugar until light and fluffy. Beat in eggs one at a time, then stir in vanilla.
4. Add half of the dry Ingredients to the butter mixture and stir until just combined; stir in the sour cream and lemon zest until just combined.
5. Add remaining dry Ingredients and stir until just combined.
6. Divide batter evenly between the prepared pans and bake for 25 to 30 minutes, or until a toothpick inserted into the center comes out clean.
7. Allow cakes to cool completely on a wire rack before frosting.

Frosting:
1. In a large bowl, beat mascarpone and heavy cream together until light and fluffy. Gradually beat in powdered sugar until desired sweetness is reached.
2. Spread frosting between the layers and over the top and sides of the cake.

Nutrition Information:
Per serving: Calories: 456; Total Fat: 22g; Saturated fat: 13g; Cholesterol: 104mg; Sodium: 135mg; Carbohydrates: 56g; Protein: 5g Fiber: 1g; Sugar: 37g

93. lemon and basil olive oil cake

Lemon and Basil Olive Oil Cake
Serving: 8
Preparation Time: 15 minutes
Cooking Time: 45 minutes

Ingredients:
- 2 cups all-purpose flour
- 2 teaspoons baking powder
- 1/2 teaspoon baking soda

- 1/2 teaspoon salt
- 3 large eggs
- 1/2 cup granulated sugar
- 1/2 cup light brown sugar
- 1/2 cup extra-virgin olive oil
- 1/2 cup freshly squeezed lemon juice
- 1/4 cup freshly chopped basil
- 1 teaspoon zest of lemon

Instructions:
1. Preheat oven to 350F/175C. Grease and flour one 9-inch baking pan.
2. In a medium bowl, whisk together the flour, baking powder, baking soda and salt.
3. In a large bowl, whisk together the eggs and sugars until pale and creamy. Add the olive oil, lemon juice, lemon zest and basil, whisking until fully incorporated.
4. Slowly add the dry Ingredients to the wet Ingredients and continue to whisk until combined.
5. Pour the batter into the prepared baking pan.
6. Bake in the preheated oven for 40-45 minutes, or until a cake tester or toothpick inserted into the center of the cake comes out clean.
7. Let the cake cool for 10 minutes before turning out onto a wire rack to cool completely.

Nutrition Information:
Calories: 298
Total Fat: 11.5g
Protein: 5.5g
Carbohydrates: 42.4g
Cholesterol: 66mg
Sodium: 224mg
Sugar: 22.7g

94. lemon and blackberry yogurt cake

This light and refreshing Lemon and Blackberry Yogurt Cake is the perfect desert to cool off during hot days. Serve it chilled with a dollop of whipped cream, or add a bit of almond granola for some crunch.

Serving: Serves 8
Preparation Time: 10 minutes
Ready Time: 40 minutes

Ingredients:
- 2 cups plain or lemon flavored yogurt
- 1/2 cup vegetable oil
- 2 eggs
- 1 cup sugar
- 2 teaspoon lemon zest
- 2 teaspoon vanilla extract
- 2 1/2 cups all-purpose flour
- 2 teaspoon baking powder
- 1 teaspoon baking soda
- 1/2 teaspoon salt
- 1 cup fresh blackberries

Instructions:
1. Preheat the oven to 350°F (175°C). Grease a 9-inch round cake pan and line the bottom with parchment paper.
2. In a large bowl, mix together the yogurt, oil, eggs, sugar, lemon zest, and vanilla extract until blended.
3. In a separate bowl, sift together the flour, baking powder, baking soda, and salt. Add this to the wet Ingredients and mix until just combined. Gently fold in the blackberries.
4. Pour the batter into the prepared cake pan and bake for 35-40 minutes, or until a toothpick comes out clean.
5. Allow the cake to cool for 10 minutes before turning out onto a serving plate and cooling completely before serving.

Nutrition Information: Per Serving (1/8 of the cake): 344 calories, 19 grams fat, 36 grams carbohydrates, 4 grams protein.

95. lemon and carrot bundt cake

This deliciously sweet and tangy Lemon and Carrot Bundt Cake is a perfectly balanced combination of sweet and tart flavors. With plenty of carrots, citrus, and coconut, this cake is sure to please everyone.

Serving: 10-12
Preparation Time: 15 minutes
Ready Time: 1 hour

Ingredients:
- 2 cups all-purpose flour
- 2 teaspoons baking powder
- 1 teaspoon baking soda
- 1 teaspoon ground cinnamon
- 1 teaspoon salt
- 3/4 cup white sugar
- 1/2 cup brown sugar
- 1/2 cup vegetable oil
- 1/2 cup strained lemon juice
- 2 eggs
- 2 cups grated carrots
- 1/2 cup sweetened flaked coconut (optional)

Instructions:
1. Preheat oven to 350F. Grease and lightly flour a 12 cup Bundt pan.
2. In a medium bowl, whisk together the flour, baking powder, baking soda, cinnamon, and salt. Set aside.
3. In the bowl of a stand mixer, beat together the oil, sugars, lemon juice, and eggs.
4. Add the dry Ingredients to the wet Ingredients, Beat until blended. Mix in the grated carrots and flaked coconut, stirring until evenly incorporated.
5. Pour the batter into the prepared Bundt pan, smoothing the top.
6. Bake for 40-45 minutes, or until a tester inserted in the cake comes out clean. Allow the cake to cool in the pan for 10 minutes before inverting onto a serving plate.

Nutrition Information:
Calories: 255, Fat: 11.9 g, Carbohydrates: 33.9 g, Protein: 2.6 g, Cholesterol: 35.2 mg, Sodium: 258.3 mg

96. lemon and coconut bundt cake

Lemon and Coconut Bundt Cake
Serving: 8
Preparation time: 10 minutes
Ready time: 1 hour

Ingredients.
1 cup butter, melted
1 ½ cup granulated sugar
3 eggs, room temperature
Zest of two lemons
2 ½ cups all-purpose flour
2 teaspoons baking powder
½ teaspoon salt
1 cup whole milk, room temperature
1 teaspoon coconut extract
2 cups shredded coconut

Instructions:
1. Preheat oven to 350 degrees F. Grease a 10-inch bundt pan with butter and set aside.
2. In a large bowl, mix together melted butter and sugar until light and fluffy.
3. Add eggs, one at a time, and mix until combined.
4. Add lemon zest and mix until incorporated.
5. In a separate bowl, sift together flour, baking powder, and salt.
6. Alternately add dry Ingredients and milk to butter-sugar mixture, beginning and ending with dry Ingredients.
7. Stir in coconut extract and shredded coconut until just combined.
8. Transfer batter to prepared bundt pan and bake for 50-55 minutes, or until a cake tester comes out clean.
9. Cool for 15 minutes, then turn out onto a wire rack to cool completely.

Nutrition Information:
Serving Size: 1 slice (about 1" thick)
Calories: 441 kcal
Total Fat: 22.3 g
Saturated Fat: 13.85 g
Cholesterol: 109.5 mg
Sodium: 317 mg

Carbohydrates: 57.6 g
Fiber: 1.6 g
Sugar: 37.3 g
Protein: 5.3 g

97. lemon and grapefruit drizzle cake

Lemon and Grapefruit Drizzle Cake
Serving: 8-10
Preparation Time: 30 minutes
Ready Time: 1 hour

Ingredients:
1 3/4 cups all-purpose flour
2 1/4 teaspoons baking powder
1/2 teaspoon salt
1/2 cup (1 stick) unsalted butter, room temperature
1 cup granulated sugar
3 large eggs
3/4 cup freshly squeezed lemon juice
1/2 cup freshly squeezed grapefruit juice
1/4 teaspoon pure vanilla extract
2 tablespoons finely grated lemon zest
2 tablespoons finely grated grapefruit zest
Frosting
2 tablespoons grapefruit juice
2 tablespoons granulated sugar

Instructions:
1. Preheat the oven to 350 F and grease and flour two 9-inch round cake pans.
2. In a medium bowl, whisk together the flour, baking powder, and salt.
3. In a large bowl, cream together the butter and sugar with an electric mixer until fluffy.
4. Beat in the eggs one at a time, then add the lemon juice, grapefruit juice, and vanilla and beat until combined.
5. Gradually add the dry Ingredients and beat until smooth.
6. Fold in the lemon zest and grapefruit zest.

7. Divide the batter evenly between the two prepared pans.
8. Bake for 25-30 minutes or until a toothpick comes out clean.
9. Cool the cakes on a wire rack for 10 minutes.
10. Meanwhile, prepare the frosting by combining the grapefruit juice with the sugar in a small saucepan over medium heat.
11. Bring to a boil, then reduce the heat and simmer for 5 minutes until thickened.
12. Remove from the heat and let cool.
13. Drizzle the cooled frosting over the warm cakes.
14. Cool completely before serving.

Nutrition Information:
Calories: 242, Fat: 10g, Saturated Fat: 6g, Cholesterol: 68mg, Sodium: 168, Fiber: 1g, Sugars: 20g

98. lemon and lavender pound cake

Lemon and Lavender Pound Cake
Serving: 10-12
Preparation Time: 25 minutes
Ready Time: 2 hours

Ingredients:
- 4 large eggs
- 1 ½ cups granulated sugar
- 1 ½ cups butter, softened
- 1 teaspoon lavender buds
- 2 tablespoons freshly squeezed lemon juice
- 2 teaspoons baking powder
- 3 ½ cups all-purpose flour
- ¼ teaspoon salt
- ½ cup heavy cream
- 1 teaspoon grated lemon zest
- 2 teaspoons vanilla extract

Instructions:
1. Preheat oven to 350°F. Grease and flour a 10-inch bundt pan.
2. In a medium bowl, beat together eggs and sugar until light and fluffy.

3. Add in butter, lavender buds, lemon juice, baking powder, flour, salt, cream, lemon zest, and vanilla extract. Beat until smooth.
4. Pour mixture into prepared pan and bake for 50-60 minutes, or until a toothpick inserted in the center comes out clean.
5. Allow cake to cool for 10 minutes before turning it out onto a cooling rack. Let cool completely before serving.

Nutrition Information per Serving (1 slice):
Calories: 270; Total Fat: 15g; Saturated Fat: 9g; Cholesterol: 75mg; Sodium: 160mg; Carbohydrates: 31g; Fiber: 1g; Sugar: 17g; Protein: 3g

99. lemon and raspberry swirl cake

Indulge in the delightful combination of tangy lemon and sweet raspberries with this irresistible Lemon and Raspberry Swirl Cake. The vibrant swirls of raspberry jam running through the moist and zesty lemon cake create a visually stunning dessert that is sure to impress. Whether you're celebrating a special occasion or simply craving a scrumptious treat, this cake is a perfect choice.
Serving: 10-12 servings
Preparation time: 20 minutes
Ready time: 1 hour 30 minutes (including baking and cooling time)

Ingredients:
For the cake:
- 2 cups all-purpose flour
- 2 teaspoons baking powder
- 1/2 teaspoon baking soda
- 1/4 teaspoon salt
- 1 cup unsalted butter, softened
- 1 1/2 cups granulated sugar
- 4 large eggs
- Zest of 2 lemons
- Juice of 1 lemon
- 1 teaspoon vanilla extract
- 1 cup buttermilk
For the raspberry swirl:
- 1/2 cup raspberry jam

For the glaze:
- 1 cup powdered sugar
- 2 tablespoons lemon juice

Instructions:
1. Preheat your oven to 350°F (175°C). Grease and flour a 9-inch (23 cm) round cake pan, or line it with parchment paper for easy removal.
2. In a medium bowl, whisk together the flour, baking powder, baking soda, and salt. Set aside.
3. In a large mixing bowl, cream together the softened butter and granulated sugar until light and fluffy. This should take about 3-4 minutes.
4. Add the eggs one at a time, beating well after each addition. Mix in the lemon zest, lemon juice, and vanilla extract.
5. Gradually add the dry Ingredients to the butter mixture, alternating with the buttermilk. Begin and end with the dry Ingredients, mixing just until combined. Do not overmix.
6. Pour half of the batter into the prepared cake pan. Spoon dollops of raspberry jam onto the batter and swirl it gently using a knife or skewer.
7. Add the remaining batter on top and repeat the swirling process with the raspberry jam.
8. Bake in the preheated oven for 45-50 minutes, or until a toothpick inserted into the center of the cake comes out clean.
9. Remove the cake from the oven and allow it to cool in the pan for 10 minutes. Then transfer it to a wire rack to cool completely.
10. While the cake is cooling, prepare the glaze by whisking together the powdered sugar and lemon juice until smooth. Adjust the consistency by adding more sugar or lemon juice if needed.
11. Once the cake has cooled, drizzle the glaze over the top. Let the glaze set for a few minutes before slicing and serving.

Nutrition Information:
(Note: The following values are approximate and may vary depending on specific Ingredients used and serving sizes.)
- Serving size: 1 slice (assuming 12 servings)
- Calories: 350
- Total fat: 15g
- Saturated fat: 9g
- Cholesterol: 85mg
- Sodium: 200mg

- Total carbohydrates: 52g
- Fiber: 1g
- Sugar: 33g
- Protein: 4g

Enjoy your delightful Lemon and Raspberry Swirl Cake!

100. lemon and thyme polenta cake

Lemon and Thyme Polenta Cake is a fragrant and delicate Italian cake that is perfect for any occasion. Its light flavor makes it ideal for a summertime dessert. The thyme brings a special earthy flavor to the cake, while the lemon provides a zesty and refreshing element to the mix.

Serving: Serves 8
Preparation time: 15 minutes
Ready time: 1 hour

Ingredients:
- 2 cups all-purpose flour
- 1 cup polenta
- 1/2 cup sugar
- Zest of 2 lemons
- 1 packet baking powder
- 1/2 teaspoon salt
- 3 eggs
- 1 cup melted butter
- 1/2 cup milk
- 2 tablespoons fresh thyme, finely chopped

Instructions:
1. Preheat the oven to 350°F. Grease and flour a 9-inch round cake pan.
2. In a medium bowl, mix together the flour, polenta, sugar, lemon zest, baking powder, and salt.
3. In a separate bowl, whisk together the eggs, melted butter, and milk.
4. Add the wet Ingredients to the dry Ingredients and mix until just combined.
5. Fold in the chopped thyme.
6. Pour the batter into the prepared pan.

7. Bake for 30-35 minutes, or until a toothpick inserted into the center comes out clean.
8. Allow to cool before serving.

Nutrition Information:
Calories – 215, Fat – 8 g, Cholesterol – 46 mg, Sodium – 181 mg, Carbohydrates – 30 g, Protein – 3.7 g

101. lemon and white chocolate layer cake with raspberry filling

Lemon and White Chocolate Layer Cake with Raspberry Filling
Serving: 8-10
Preparation Time: 25 minutes
Ready Time: 1 hour 20 minutes

Ingredients:
- 8 ounces almond flour
- 1 teaspoon baking powder
- 1 teaspoon salt
- 6 tablespoons butter, melted
- 4 large eggs
- 1/2 cup cashew milk
- 1 teaspoon vanilla extract
- 1/2 cup white sugar
- zest of 1 lemon
- 3/4 cup white chocolate chips
- 1/4 cup raspberry jam

Instructions:
1. Preheat the oven to 375°F. Grease two 9-inch baking pans and line with parchment paper.
2. In a medium-sized bowl, whisk together the almond flour, baking powder, and salt.
3. In a large bowl, whisk together the melted butter, eggs, cashew milk, vanilla, sugar, and lemon zest until light and fluffy.
4. Add the dry Ingredients to the wet Ingredients and stir until combined.

5. Divide the batter evenly between the prepared pans and spread evenly.
6. Scatter the white chocolate chips over the top of the batter in the pans.
7. Bake for 20 minutes, or until a toothpick inserted into the center comes out clean.
8. Allow the cakes to cool in the pans for 10 minutes. Meanwhile, prepare the raspberry filling.
9. In a medium-sized bowl, stir together the raspberry jam and 1 teaspoon of water.
10. To assemble the cake, place one layer on a serving plate or cake stand. Top with the raspberry filling and spread evenly. Layer the second cake on top.
11. Serve immediately. Enjoy!

Nutrition Information:
Calories: 330, Total Fat: 17.6g, Saturated Fat: 8.2g, Sodium: 279mg, Carbohydrates: 35.5g, Fiber: 2.2g, Protein: 5.4g.

102. lemon ricotta bundt cake

Lemon Ricotta Bundt Cake
Serving: 8
Preparation Time: 10 minutes
Ready Time: 1 hour

Ingredients:
- 2 cups all-purpose flour
- 1 teaspoon baking powder
- 1/2 teaspoon baking soda
- Pinch of salt
- 1/2 cup (1 stick) unsalted butter, melted and cooled
- 1 1/4 cups granulated sugar
- 2 large eggs
- 1/2 cup full-fat ricotta cheese
- 2 tablespoons freshly grated lemon zest
- 1 teaspoon pure vanilla extract
- 1/4 cup fresh lemon juice (from 1 large lemon)
- 3/4 cup whole milk

- Powdered sugar, for serving (optional)

Instructions:
1. Preheat the oven to 350°F. Grease and flour an 8-inch Bundt pan.
2. In a medium bowl, whisk together the flour, baking powder, baking soda, and salt.
3. In a separate bowl, whisk together the melted butter, granulated sugar, eggs, ricotta cheese, lemon zest, vanilla extract, and lemon juice until combined.
Add the dry Ingredients to the wet Ingredients and mix until just combined.
4. Pour the batter into the prepared Bundt pan and bake for 45-50 minutes, or until a toothpick comes out clean.
5. Let the cake cool in the pan for 10 minutes before inverting it onto a platter. Dust with powdered sugar if desired.

Nutrition Information:
Calories: 352, Fat: 11.6g, Saturated Fat: 6.5g, Cholesterol: 74mg, Sodium: 181.3mg, Carbohydrates: 54g, Fiber: 0.9g, Sugar: 30.2g, Protein: 6.3g

103. lemon and strawberry cream cheese pound cake

Lemon and Strawberry Cream Cheese Pound Cake
Serving: 10 to 12 servings
Preparation time: 25 minutes
Ready time: 1 hour 25 minutes

Ingredients:
- 2 1/2 cups all-purpose flour
- 2 teaspoons baking powder
- 1/2 teaspoon salt
- 2 sticks (1 cup) unsalted butter, at room temperature
- 8 ounces cream cheese, at room temperature
- 2 cups sugar
- 4 large eggs
- Zest of 1 lemon
- 2 teaspoons pure vanilla extract
- 1/2 cup buttermilk

- 2 cups fresh or frozen strawberries, diced

Instructions:
1. Preheat the oven to 350 degrees F and lightly grease and flour a 9-inch tube pan.
2. In a medium bowl, whisk together the flour, baking powder and salt.
3. In a large bowl, cream together the butter, cream cheese and sugar until light and fluffy. Beat in the eggs one at a time, scraping down the sides of the bowl after each addition. Beat in the lemon zest and vanilla extract.
4. Alternately add the dry Ingredients and the buttermilk to the creamed mixture, beginning and ending with the dry Ingredients and mixing until just combined. Gently fold in the diced strawberries with a spatula.
5. Pour the batter into the prepared pan and spread evenly. Bake for 1 hour to 1 hour and 15 minutes, or until a tester comes out clean. Allow to cool before removing from the pan.

Nutrition Information: Calories 345; Protein 4g; Carbohydrates 47.5g; Fat 16.2g; Sodium 140mg; Cholesterol 91mg.

CONCLUSION

Luscious Lemon Cakes is the perfect cookbook for anyone who loves the tangy and sweet taste of lemon. With over 100 delicious recipes, this cookbook provides a wide variety of lemon cake options that will satisfy any sweet tooth. Whether you are looking for a simple lemon loaf or a more complex layer cake, Luscious Lemon Cakes has got you covered.

One of the standout features of this cookbook is the depth and variety of recipes. The cookbook includes recipes for classic lemon cakes like lemon pound cake and lemon bundt cake, as well as more unique recipes like lemon poppyseed and lemon lavender. Each recipe is well-written and easy to follow, making it accessible to even novice bakers.

In addition to the recipes, the cookbook also includes beautiful full-color photos of each dish, making it easy to visualize what each dish should look like. This is especially helpful when it comes to more complex cakes, like layer cakes or souffles.

One of the best aspects of this cookbook is its versatility. The recipes are perfect for any occasion, whether you are baking for a special celebration or just looking to satisfy a sweet craving. Some of the recipes are quick and easy to make, perfect for a weekday treat, while others are more complex and time-consuming, making them ideal for a special occasion.

Another great feature of this cookbook is the tips and tricks provided throughout the book. From advice on how to properly measure ingredients to tips for decorating cakes, these tips will help you achieve the best possible results. These tips are especially useful for novice bakers who may be new to working with lemon in their baking.

Overall, Luscious Lemon Cakes is a fantastic cookbook that is sure to satisfy any sweet tooth. With its variety of recipes, helpful tips, and beautiful photos, it is a must-have for anyone who loves baking with lemon. So go ahead, grab a copy of Luscious Lemon Cakes and start baking today!

Printed in Dunstable, United Kingdom